Zany Wooden Toys that Whiz, Spin, Pop and Fly

by Bob Gilsdorf

FOX CHAPEL
PUBLISHING

ABOUT THE AUTHOR

Bob Gilsdorf was born in Minnesota and lived there through the sixth grade, when he moved to Phoenix, Arizona, to thaw out, remaining there through college. After discovering the climate and location of Colorado Springs was comfortably between those two extremes, Bob settled there, married a beautiful lady, and started a family. Bob has five wonderful boys whose creativity and interests continually introduce him to new adventures.

Bob's father, who was always building something, introduced woodworking to Bob at a young age. Bob spent many hours looking at the toy books his mom gave him trying to decide what to make. Over the years, he built wooden toys, dollhouses, and gifts for his brothers, sisters, parents, and cousins. Shop class in elementary school taught him the basics of drafting and woodworking, and he continued studying those subjects in high school and college. Bob now works as an engineering manager for a semiconductor company that makes microcontrollers and memory chips, but he continues to make toys, furniture, and other wooden projects as time permits.

www.TheToyInventorsWorkshop.com

DEDICATION

To my beautiful wife, Peggy: an amazing mom and my best friend. To our five adventurous boys (Ben, Jeremy, Adam, Sawyer, and Noah) who inspired these projects with their cute smiles, fun-filled spirits, and their simple requests: "Can we go make a toy?" And, to my creative Mom and Dad for their countless, patient hours teaching me the skills necessary for doing this stuff and allowing me to make my own mistakes.

ACKNOWLEDGMENTS

A dusty notebook and some rough-cut toys could only be turned into a book by an immensely talented group of people like Peg Couch (Acquisition Editor), Kerri Landis (Assistant Editor), Troy Thorne (Creative Director), Lindsay Hess (Book Designer), Scott Kriner (Photographer), and Dan Clarke (Book Designer). They each added their vision and expertise to "invent" this book.

I would also like to acknowledge William Clark for lending his drafting expertise to bring several of the toys to life on a piece of paper.

Don't shoot people or animals

There are many toys in this book that launch objects through the air or shoot objects across the ground. Be extremely careful not to aim at any people or animals. If you want to shoot at something, line up some action figures or cans and bottles. You could even create your own wooden target, or build the Hockey Man Target on page 115.

ISBN 978-1-56523-394-2

Library of Congress Cataloging-in-Publication Data

Gilsdorf, Bob, 1963-

Zany wooden toys that whiz, spin, pop, and fly / by Bob Gilsdorf. -- 1st ed.

　p. cm.

ISBN: 978-1-56523-394-2

1. Wooden toy making. I. Title.

TX773.G485 2009

745.592--dc22　　　　　　　　　　　　　2009013828

To learn more about the other great books from Fox Chapel Publishing, or to find a retailer near you, call toll-free 800-457-9112 or visit us at *www.FoxChapelPublishing.com*.

Note to Authors: We are always looking for talented authors to write new books in our area of woodworking, design, and related crafts. Please send a brief letter describing your idea to Acquisition Editor, 1970 Broad Street, East Petersburg, PA 17520.

Printed in China
First printing: August 2009

Preface

Welcome to my notebook. This is where my inventions start. I hope that after reading through my notebook and seeing how I create new toys, you will be inspired to make your own.

My inventions start as just a thought or a question that I capture by quickly jotting down a few notes. I find this to be very useful because ideas are sensitive little things and will quickly fly off if you don't spend a little time with them. After the idea is captured, a little engineering and experimenting are needed. This is where you think through the idea on paper and let the pencil do most of the work—perhaps sketching some designs or doing a little math to see if it will really work. All of this goes in the notebook.

Once you have a plan for what your invention will do and what it should look like, then it's time to head to the workbench. This is where you lift your idea off the paper and into your hands—it's where your invention becomes real.

Unfortunately, this is also where the mistakes are found. There are always mistakes, but inventors get used to making mistakes. That is part of the fun of inventing something. So it's time to go back into the notebook to write down what worked and what didn't work. After a little more hard thinking, it's back to the shop with your new ideas.

Finally, you put in that last nail, attach the rubber band, push the button, and—eureka—your invention does exactly what you wanted it to do. It actually works. Five minutes ago, you were starting to think you were wasting your time, but now it all seems worthwhile. Pat yourself on the back, and then go show your family and friends your amazing new invention. Guaranteed, they've never seen anything like it, because you invented it.

As a final thought, just in case you (or your parents) wonder what this goofy stuff has to do with Your Future Career in the Electronic Age, consider this. Before being made in its current form, the iPod was sculpted from foamcore board, cardboard, tape, and fishing weights—just as each of the inventions in this book were made in rough experimental forms before the final polished ones, and just as any toys you invent will progress from an idea to a finished work of art.

Go invent and have fun!

Bob

CONTENTS

INTRODUCTION

The plans for the projects are intended to help you make the toys as quickly as possible. The plans can either be copied (with enlargement) and cut out, or measured and marked directly on the wood. The dashed fold lines show where to fold the pattern over the edge of the wood so two sides can be marked at once. Accuracy is not too critical on most of the projects. You'll be able to see easily what pieces need to align. Pay attention to notes and helpful hints to make the projects go more smoothly. Also, don't worry too much about having the exact supplies listed. You can use anything that works.

Step-by-Step Toys

Enter the world of toy making with these two photo-packed step-by-step projects. The Warp-Speed Penny Shooter propels a penny over the floor, up a ramp—wherever you want. The Tissue-Launching Crossbow is a hygienic way to supply your favorite sick person with tissues.

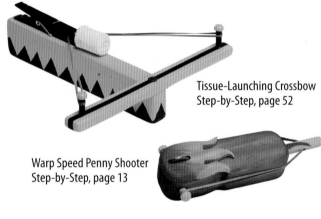

Tissue-Launching Crossbow
Step-by-Step, page 52

Warp Speed Penny Shooter
Step-by-Step, page 13

Shooters, page 10

These six projects will flick, push, spin, or kick an object over a flat surface. Use these toys to smack a wooden puck, ball, or coin.

Launchers, page 50

Five projects that flip, shoot, and fire objects through the air. Build toys that propel quarters, ping-pong balls, and more.

*Zany Wooden Toys that **Whiz, Spin, Pop,** and **Fly***

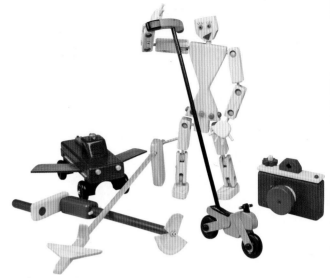

Games, page 86

These six projects are easy to use in a game—add a ball, make some goalposts, follow rules you know, or create your own. Create a miniature baseball, hockey, or croquet game.

Toys, page 122

These six projects will inspire your imagination. Make your very own camera that can capture the real and the imaginary, a robot to carry out your bidding, and much more.

Gumball Machines, page 162

These four projects will have you wondering how you ever found gratification turning a knob to get a gumball. Now you can smack and catapult gumballs with these interactive toys.

Woodworking Basics, page 194

Get the scoop on selecting wood, making cuts, creating connectors, and other basic skills for building toys. With special tips for working with kids.

SHOOTERS

If you're looking for an action toy that flicks, kicks, pushes, slams, or spins an object over a flat surface, you've come to the right place. This chapter begins with the Warp-Speed Penny Shooter— a fun and easy project to kick off your toy-making career. Follow the step-by-step instructions and you'll be smacking pennies across the floor in no time! Follow that up with the Thumb-Action Marble Shooter (page 24), Pool Cue Marble Shooter (page 29), Nickel Spinner (page 34), Ricochet Shooter (page 39), and U-Control Soccer Player (page 44).

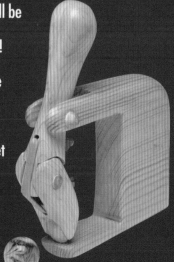

The other day, I was at the grocery store and accidentally dropped my wallet on the floor.

Before I knew it, coins were whizzing in every direction.

So, I wondered...

What kind of toy would send a coin rolling across the floor in any direction I wanted and at a high speed?

POW

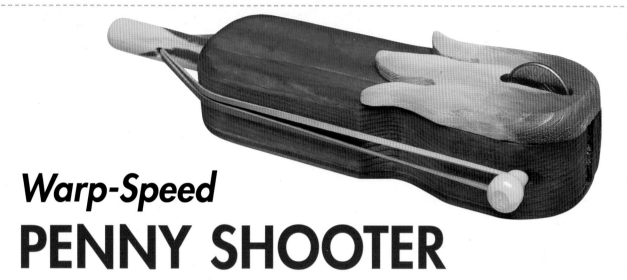

Warp-Speed
PENNY SHOOTER
STEP-BY-STEP

This is a great beginner project because you'll learn how to make straight and internal cuts, and to drill holes in flat boards and round dowels. When you're done, you'll be launching pennies across the floor and inventing all types of games to play. Then, improve your skills by building a second penny shooter without using any measurements. To do this, drill the hole for the ramrod as deep as you want and then cut off the board about a half-inch longer (about the width of your finger). Use a penny to mark how wide and long you need to make the slots. Guesstimate everything else and you'll have your second toy in no time at all.

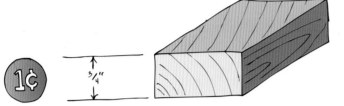

Need to hold penny vertically then hit it.

The Coin: A penny is about ¾" (19mm) in diameter, which is the same width as a common pine board such as a 1 x 2. The penny also has a nice wide, smooth edge which may help it stay standing. Plus, they're cheap! Your piggy bank is probably full of them.

The RamRod: The easiest way is to push it from behind. The pusher has to be flat on the end, sturdy, and much wider than a penny. The flat end of a dowel could be used as a ramrod.

PoweRing the RamRod: I could use a spring, but rubber bands are easier to find and easy to use. I'll go with a rubber band.

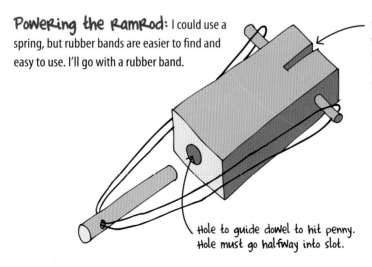

FoR the coin to Roll, it will have to stay on its edge. If I cut a slot out of a piece of Wood it will stay upRight.

Hole to guide dowel to hit penny. Hole must go halfway into slot.

Warp-Speed Penny Shooter

Top Coin Slot

Anchor Pin

Coin Slot

Base

Rubber Band

RamRod
Guide Hole

Bottom

RamRod

Nails

The money really
will be rolling in with
this super shooter!

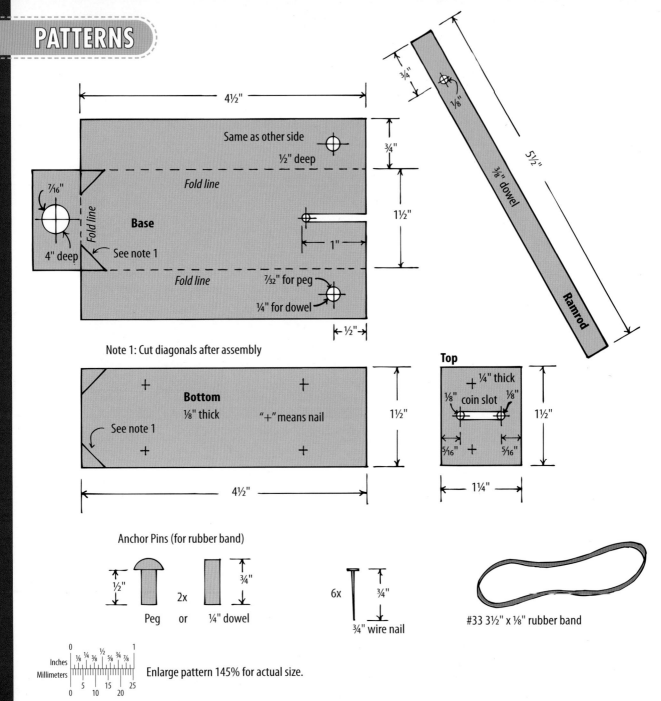

4½"

Same as other side
½" deep

¾"

Fold line

7/16"

Fold line

Base

1½"

4" deep

See note 1

1"

Fold line

7/32" for peg

¼" for dowel

½"

Note 1: Cut diagonals after assembly

+   +

Bottom
⅛" thick   "+" means nail

See note 1

1½"

+   +

4½"

3/4

⅛"

3/8" dowel

5½"

Ramrod

Top

¼" thick

⅛" coin slot ⅛"

1½"

5/16"   5/16"

1¼"

Anchor Pins (for rubber band)

½"   ¾"

2x

Peg   or   ¼" dowel

6x   ¾"

¾" wire nail

#33 3½" x ⅛" rubber band

0   1
Inches ⅛ ¼ ⅜ ½ ⅝ ¾ ⅞
Millimeters
0   5   10   15   20   25

Enlarge pattern 145% for actual size.

Zany Wooden Toys that Whiz, Spin, Pop, and Fly

- ☑ ¾" (19mm) x 1½" (38mm) x 4½" (114mm) pine board for base
- ☑ ¼" (6mm) x 1¼" (32mm) x 1½" (38mm) plywood for coin slot
- ☑ ⅛" (3mm) x 1½" (38mm) x 4½" (114mm) plywood for bottom
- ☑ ⅜" (10mm) dowel, 5½" (140mm) long for ramrod
- ☑ ¼" (6mm) dowel, 1½" (38mm) long for anchor pins
- ☑ ¾" (19mm) wire brad nails, 6
- ☑ #33, 3½" (89mm) x ⅛" (3mm) rubber band (use whatever you have)
- ☑ Penny
- ☑ Coping saw
- ☑ Drill
- ☑ ⅛" (3mm), ¼" (6mm), and ⁷⁄₁₆" (11mm) drill bits
- ☑ Hammer
- ☑ Awl or nail for marking drill holes
- ☑ Vise
- ☑ Square
- ☑ Pencil
- ☑ Scissors
- ☑ Masking tape
- ☑ Thin wire for pulling rubber band

Engineering Advice:

The old saying is true. If at first you don't succeed, try and try again. Below is a look at my first prototype:

Problem: Rubber band is wearing out at the back corner.

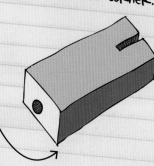

Solution: Angle the back corners so they are not so sharp.

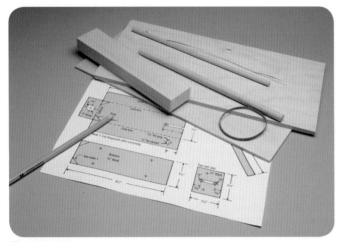

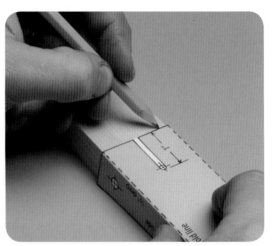

1 Collect all of the supplies listed on the Materials and Tools List and make copies of the patterns. (Alternatively, you can measure and mark all of the cut lines and hole locations.)

2 Cut out the patterns following the bold lines. Fold the pattern for the base along the dashed lines. Place the patterns on the wood and mark the shapes.

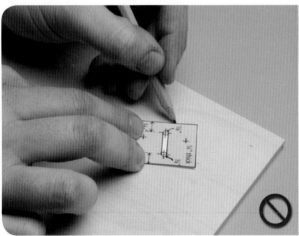

3 Make sure you position the patterns on the wood to minimize waste and the number of cuts you will need to make. The setup shown on the left requires more work because several long cuts are needed. The setup on the right is easier because only two cuts are needed.

Zany Wooden Toys that **Whiz, Spin, Pop,** *and* **Fly**

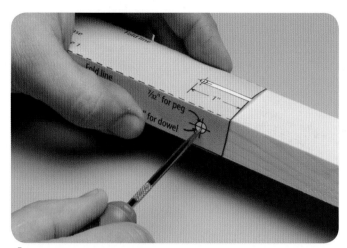

4 Use the awl or nail to poke the centers for the four holes that will be drilled in the base and the two holes for the internal cut in the top coin slot.

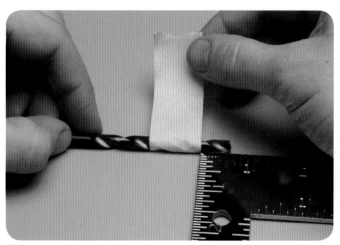

5 Wrap masking tape around the ¼" (6mm) drill bit about ½" (13mm) from the end. This will mark the depth of the holes for the ¼" (6mm) anchor pins. Do this for the ⁷⁄₁₆" (11mm) drill bit to mark a depth of 4" (102mm).

6 Drill the ¼" (6mm) holes on both sides of the base to a depth of ½" (13mm). Use the tape to show you where to stop.

*Zany Wooden Toys that **Whiz, Spin, Pop,** and **Fly***

7 Drill the ⅛" (3mm) hole from the top of the base. This hole goes completely through the wood, so put a piece of scrap wood underneath to prevent damaging the drill or tabletop. Also, drill the two ⅛" (3mm) holes for the coin slot in the top piece.

8 Drill the ⁷⁄₁₆" (11mm) hole to a depth of 4" (102mm). Drilling the hole straight down the middle of the base is important so the ramrod will go into the middle of the slot and hit the penny. Take extra time to make sure the drill bit is parallel to the front and sides.

9 Mark and cut the ⅜" (10mm) dowel for the ramrod and the ¼" (6mm) dowel for the two anchor pins. Drill a ⅛" (3mm) hole about ¼" (6mm) from the end of the ⅜" (10mm) dowel for the rubber band. You can either clamp the dowel or place it on a piece of scrap wood.

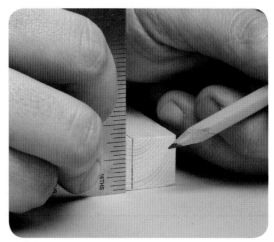

10 Clamp the base horizontally in the vise and use the coping saw to remove any excess. Use scrap wood on both sides of your piece to prevent the vise from scratching it.

11 Use the square to mark the end of the base with lines for the slot. These will help align the coping saw.

12 Reposition the base vertically and use the coping saw to cut out the slot. Start the cut with the blade contacting only the far corner. After the cut has been started, level out the blade. Saw into the ⅛" (3mm) holes on both sides.

13 Mount the ¼" (6mm) plywood for the coin slot in the vise. Make the internal cut first. To do this, disconnect one end of the coping saw blade and pass it through the top hole. Reconnect the blade and make the two internal cuts for the coin slot. Make the two outside cuts to finish the top coin slot. **Note**—Holding the ¼" (6mm) board with your free hand will prevent it from wobbling too much and will improve the accuracy of your cut.

14 Use the coping saw to cut out the ⅛" (3mm)-thick bottom piece. Just cut the rectangular shape for now; the corners will be removed later.

The internal cut for the coin slot is not necessary; it is just for looks. If you don't have a coping saw, just make an open slot. Have the open end facing the ramrod.

15 Align the top coin slot with the base and insert a penny. The penny should fall straight through. If it doesn't, try flipping the top piece over or sanding off the edges of the slot that interfere with the penny's movement.

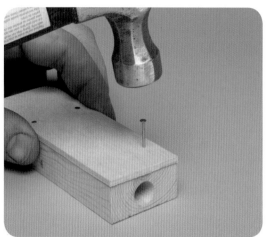

16 Flip the base over and nail the ⅛" (3mm)-thick bottom to it using four ¾" (19mm) wire brad nails.

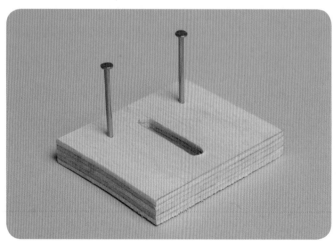

17 Start the two nails for the top by pounding them in about ⅛" (3mm). This will allow you to hold the top coin slot in alignment with the base while pounding the nails.

18 Use your index finger and thumb to feel that the edges of the top coin slot are aligned with the edges of the base. Visually check the alignment at the front and down through the slot. Pound in the nails.

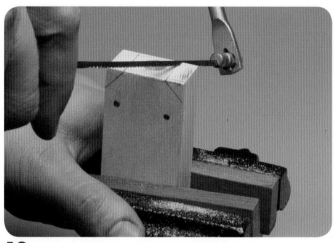

19 Now cut off the corners using the coping saw.

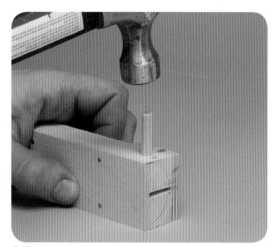

20 Pound in the ¼" (6mm) anchor pins on the left and right sides.

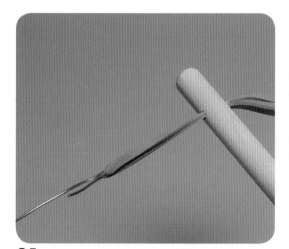

21 Make a hook on one end of the thin wire, and use it to pull the rubber band through the hole in the ⅜" (10mm) dowel.

22 Insert the dowel in the back of the base and then attach the rubber band to the ¼" (6mm) dowels. Place the toy on the floor. Set the penny in the coin slot opening. Pull back the ⅜" (10mm) dowel about an inch or two. The penny should fall into the slot. On my mark, prepare for warp speed...3...2...1...release!

Zany Wooden Toys that Whiz, Spin, Pop, and Fly

Thumb-Action
MARBLE SHOOTER

This is a fun project that will show you how to make hinges. Sometimes you want a hinge to move as much as possible, and other times, you want a hinge to stop at a certain point. This toy has both kinds. Once you figure out the basics of the hinges you can make all types of mechanisms. A special feature of this toy is that it grosses out girls... especially if you carve a fingernail on it!

The bones: I'll start by making the end of the new thumb about the same size as my real thumb, ¾" (19mm) x ¾" (19mm) x 1½" (38mm).

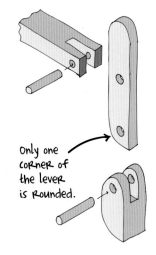

Only one corner of the lever is rounded.

The knuckles: Instead of knuckles, we'll make hinges out of wood with hinge pins made from ¼" (6mm) dowels. We'll round only one corner on the lever, so that the thumb only bends inward and not outward. In this case, a double-jointed thumb will not be helpful. But feel free to think up a toy that could use a double-jointed finger!

The muscles: A rubber band will provide all of the muscle we need. We'll attach the rubber band using an eye screw and a hook screw.

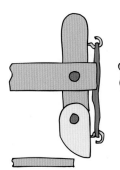
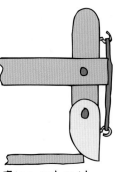
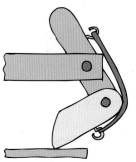

The Release mechanism: To shoot a marble, the thumbnail pushes against the inside of the index finger. Our new thumb will push against a board to build up power.

Thumb too short: No snap action

Thumb just Right: Max power

Thumb too long: Won't Release

Thumb-Action Marble Shooter

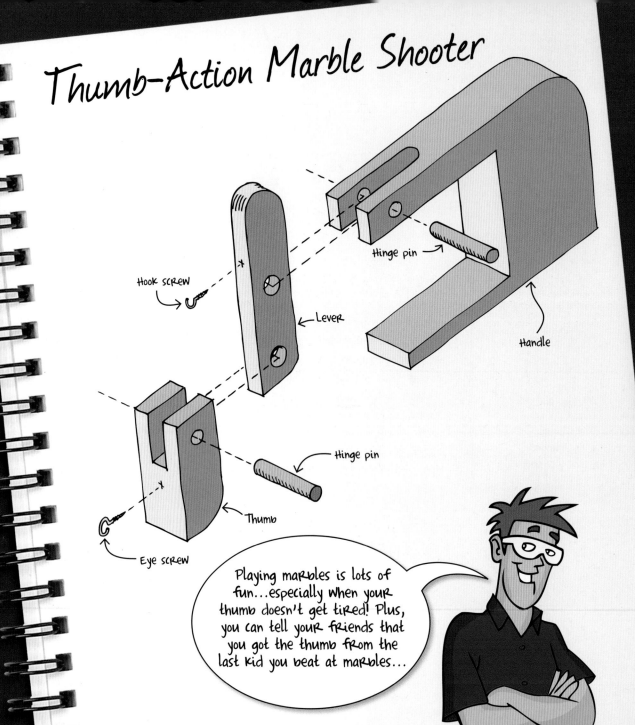

PATTERNS

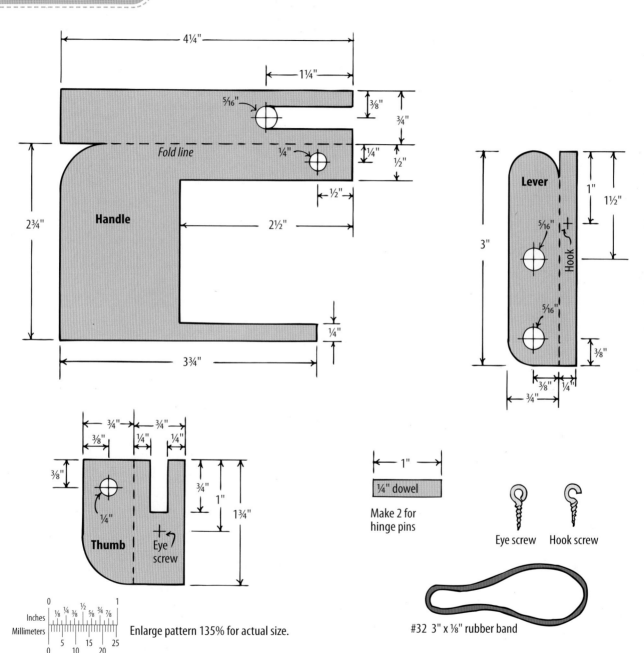

Enlarge pattern 135% for actual size.

¼" dowel

Make 2 for hinge pins

Eye screw   Hook screw

#32 3" x ⅛" rubber band

- ☑ ¾" (19mm) x 2¾" (70mm) x 4¼" (108mm) pine board for handle

- ☑ ¾" (19mm) x ¾" (19mm) x 1¾" (44mm) pine board for thumb

- ☑ ¼" (6mm) x ¾" (19mm) x 3" (76mm) pine board for lever

- ☑ ¼" (6mm) dowel, 2" (51mm) long for hinge pins

- ☑ Hook screw (can be made from screw eye)

- ☑ Eye screw

- ☑ #64, 3½" (89mm) x ¼" (6mm) Rubber band (doubled-over)

- ☑ Wooden ball or marble

- ☑ Coping saw

- ☑ Drill

- ☑ ¼" (6mm) and ⁵⁄₁₆" (8mm) drill bits

- ☑ Awl to mark locations for hook screw and eye screw

- ☑ Needle-nose pliers (or strong fingers) to screw in hook screw and eye screw

Engineering Advice:

The rubber band can get stuck in the hinge. Try twisting the rubber band so it's thicker. Also, try putting a small groove on the lever.

Check your thumb to make sure it doesn't bend backward. This will make it jam when you go to shoot a marble. Been there, done that—had to scratch my head for a while before I figured it out!

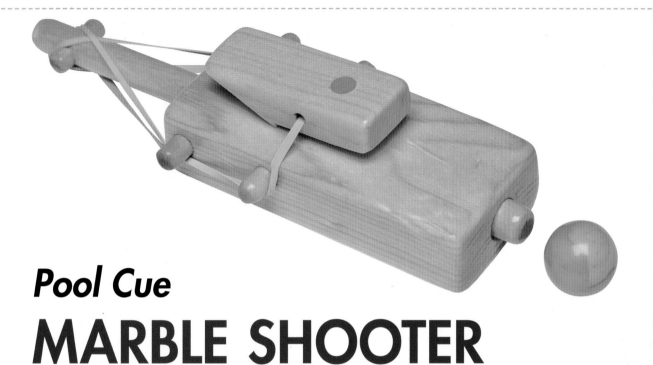

Pool Cue
MARBLE SHOOTER

Pull back and latch the pool cue, carefully aim it at your marble, tap the release latch, and—BAM!—you'll get the perfect shot every time. This may seem complicated, but it's really just a matter of making some straight cuts and drilling a few holes. Just make the shooter, and the games will invent themselves!

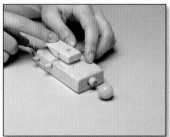
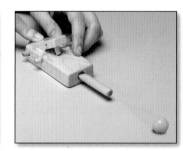

The pool cue: An obvious choice for the pool cue is a dowel. Let's choose a ⅜" (10mm) dowel to give us a wide flat area to hit the marble.

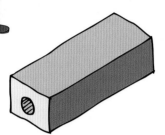

Aiming the pool cue: A hole through a block of wood will guide the pool cue.

Propulsion: Let's use a rubber band to pull the pool cue through the hole in the block of wood.

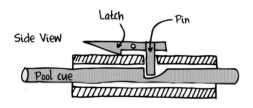

Side View

Latch · Pin

Pool cue

The latch for the pool cue: Pushing down on the end of the latch will lift the pin and release the pool cue. We'll need to put a notch in the dowel.

Game Idea: Capture or Save the χ

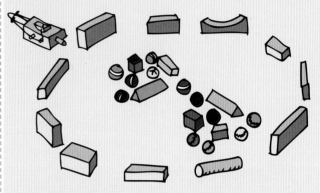

Here, X can be anything you'd want to capture or save: the treasure, the general, the alien, the monkey, the pretty pink pony, the environment, etc.

Objective:
Knock your opponent's X marble outside the ring.

Setup:
Make a 2' (610mm) diameter ring using scrap wood to mark the perimeter. Leave about 3" (76mm) between pieces. Each player colors five wooden balls and marks a sixth ball as the X. Each player then positions three scrap pieces of wood and their five colored balls around the X ball to protect it.

To Play:
Players take turns shooting a wooden ball from outside the ring (through the gaps) to try to move the opponent's X outside the ring. The first one to succeed wins the treasure, captures the general, destroys the alien, saves the monkey, finds the lost pretty pink pony—you get the idea.

Pool Cue Marble Shooter

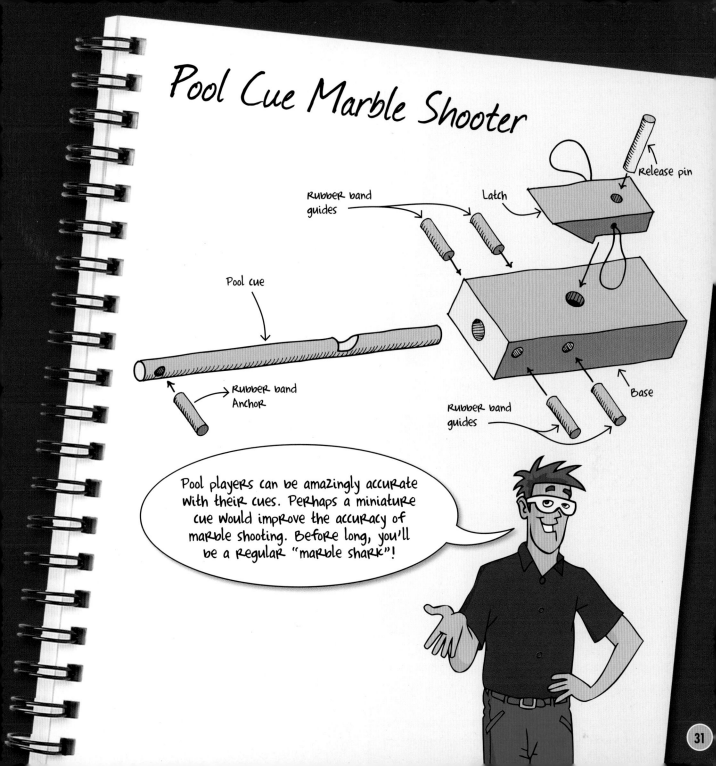

Release pin

Rubber band guides

Latch

Pool cue

Rubber band Anchor

Rubber band guides

Base

Pool players can be amazingly accurate with their cues. Perhaps a miniature cue would improve the accuracy of marble shooting. Before long, you'll be a regular "marble shark"!

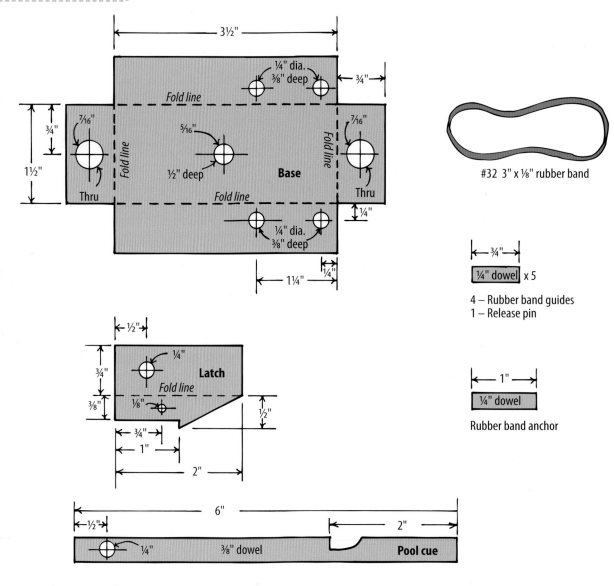

3½"

¼" dia.
⅜" deep

¾"

Fold line

7⁄16"

¾"

Fold line

5⁄16"

Fold line

1½"

½" deep

Base

7⁄16"

Fold line

Thru

Thru

¼"

Fold line

¼" dia.
⅜" deep

1¼"

¼"

#32 3" x ⅛" rubber band

¾"

¼" dowel x 5

4 – Rubber band guides
1 – Release pin

½"

¼"

¾"

Latch

Fold line

⅜"

⅛"

½"

¾"

1"

2"

1"

¼" dowel

Rubber band anchor

6"

½"

¼"

⅜" dowel

2"

Pool cue

0   1
Inches   ⅛ ¼ ⅜ ½ ⅝ ¾ ⅞
Millimeters
5 10 15 20 25
0

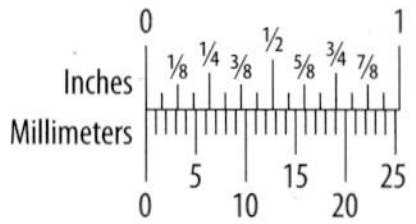

Enlarge pattern 145% for actual size.

- ☑ ³⁄₄" (19mm) x 1½" (38mm) x 3½" (89mm) pine board for base
- ☑ ³⁄₄" (19mm) x ³⁄₄" (19mm) x 2" (51mm) pine board for latch
- ☑ ³⁄₈" (10mm) dowel, 6" (152mm) long for pool cue
- ☑ ¼" (6mm) dowel, 6" (152mm) long for guides, anchor pin, and release pin
- ☑ #32, 3" (76mm) x ⅛" (3mm) rubber band
- ☑ Wooden ball or marble
- ☑ Coping saw
- ☑ Drill
- ☑ ⅛" (3mm), ¼" (6mm), ⁵⁄₁₆" (8mm), and ⁷⁄₁₆" (11mm) drill bits
- ☑ Clamp or vise for holding small pieces while cutting
- ☑ Thin wire for pulling rubber band

Engineering Advice:

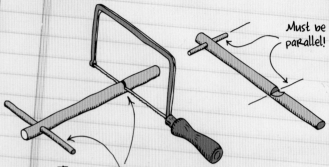

Must be parallel!

The notch in the pool cue has to be parallel to the anchor pin to keep the slot facing upward.

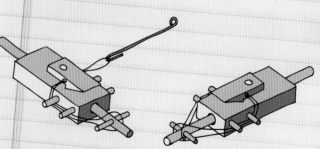

Loop the rubber band as shown. This will keep the slot in the pool cue facing upward.

Zany Wooden Toys that *Whiz, Spin, Pop,* and *Fly*

NICKEL SPINNER

This is an easy-to-make toy with only three pieces to cut out and some dowels. It uses a simple latch and hammer mechanism to send a nickel spinning across the floor. Try experimenting with hitting the nickel on its edge or toward the center. You can create games for longest spin time, accuracy, nickel battles, and who-knows-what!

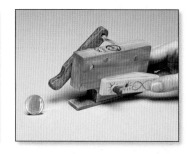

Zany Wooden Toys that *Whiz, Spin, Pop,* and *Fly*

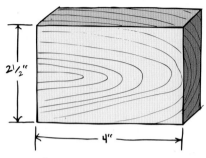

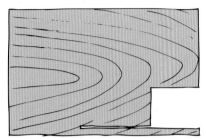

Sizing the spinner: I'd like to make the spinner about the size of my palm—not too big. So for the spinner's largest piece—the coin holder—let's use a block of wood that measures 2½" x 4" (64mm x 102mm). We'll use a nickel because it's the largest coin with a smooth edge.

Holding the coin: Cut an opening for the nickel in the block of wood. The opening should be slightly smaller than the nickel's diameter and close to the bottom of the holder. The nickel will be held in place by wedging it on end into the opening. The bottom piece should be thin and springy to help hold the nickel in place. Notice the direction of the wood grain in the drawing.

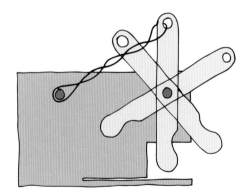

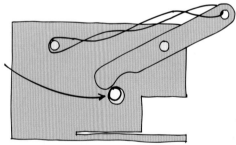

Bevel or angle the end of the latch dowel. Notice how the rubber band is placed.

Hitting the coin: The coin must be hit on its edge to get it spinning. A small rotating hammer powered by a rubber band will do the job!

Holding the hammer back: Now our contraption needs a latch to hold the hammer back until we're ready. If we drill a hole in the path of the hammer, we can then insert a dowel to keep the hammer in a cocked position. By pulling the dowel through the hole on the other side, the hammer will be released. The dowel, or release pin, will be connected to a seesaw latch so when one end is squeezed, the other end pulls the dowel through the hole and releases the hammer.

Zany Wooden Toys that Whiz, Spin, Pop, and Fly

Nickel Spinner

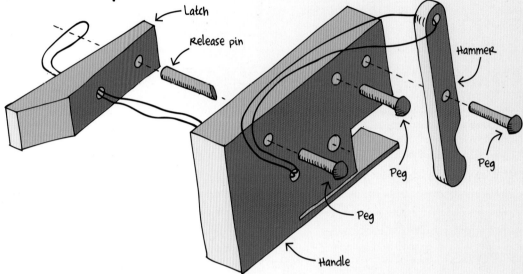

Latch

Release pin

Hammer

Peg

Peg

Peg

Handle

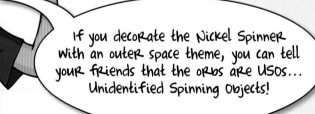

If you decorate the Nickel Spinner with an outer space theme, you can tell your friends that the orbs are USOs... Unidentified Spinning Objects!

PATTERNS

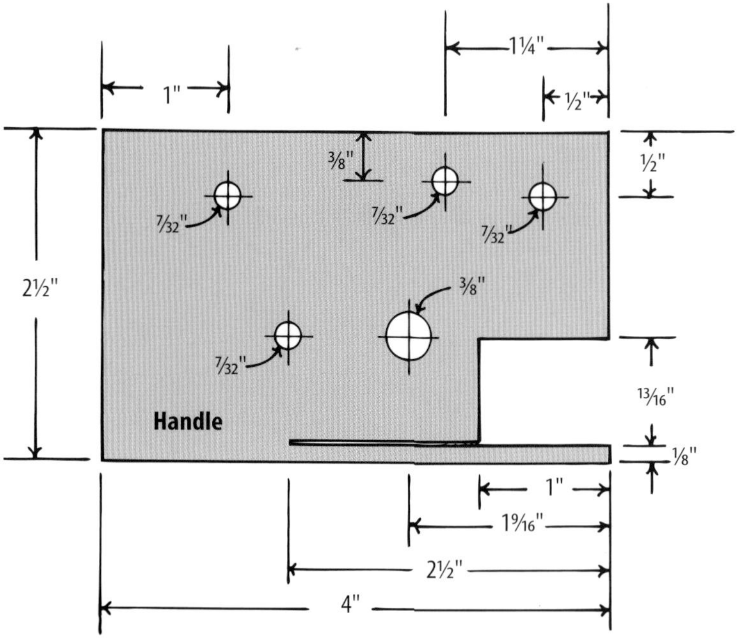
1"
1¼"
½"
⅜"
½"
7/32"
7/32"
7/32"
⅜"
2½"
7/32"
13/16"
Handle
⅛"
1"
1 9/16"
2½"
4"

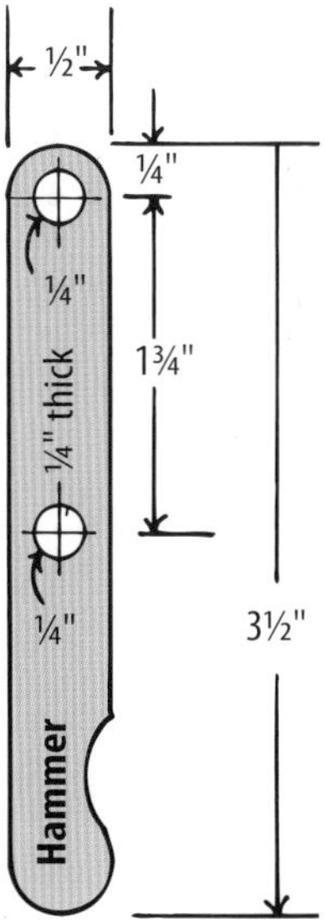
½"
¼"
¼"
1¾"
¼" thick
3½"
¼"
Hammer

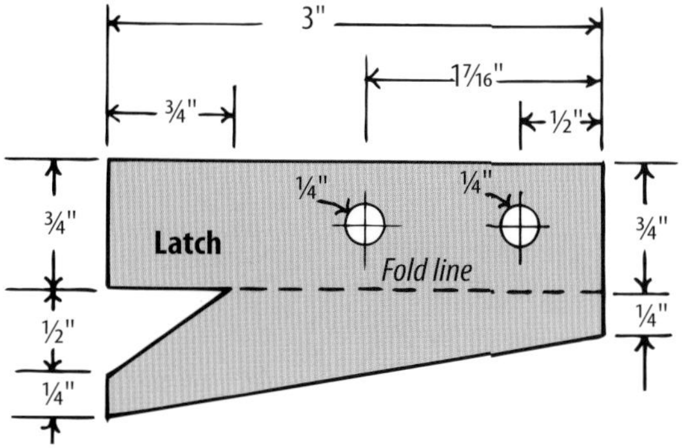
3"
1 7/16"
¾"
½"
¼"
¼"
¾"
Latch
¾"
Fold line
½"
¼"
¼"

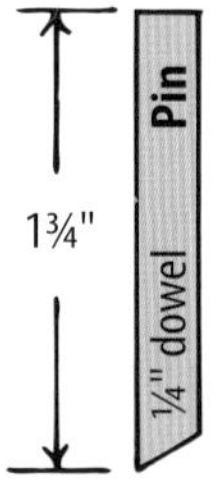
1¾"
Pin
¼" dowel

Release pin

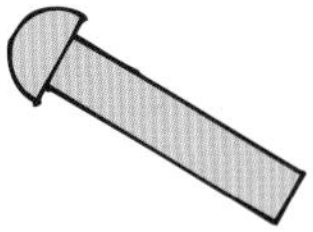

3 Pegs, 1" long
or
¼" dowel

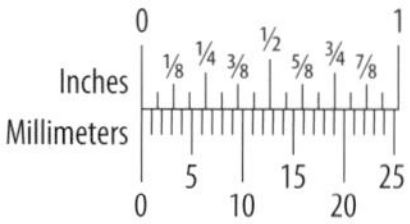
Inches
Millimeters
0
⅛
¼
⅜
½
⅝
¾
⅞
1
0
5
10
15
20
25

Enlarge pattern 145% for actual size.

MATERIALS & TOOLS

- ☑ ³⁄₄" (19mm) x 2½" (64mm) x 7" (178mm) pine board for handle and latch
- ☑ ¼" (6mm) x ½" (13mm) x 3½" (89mm) pine board or plywood for hammer
- ☑ ¼" (6mm) dowel, 2" (51mm) long for release pin
- ☑ Pegs, or 1" (25mm)-long pieces of ¼" (6mm) dowel, 3
- ☑ #33, 3½" (89mm) x ⅛" (3mm) rubber band
- ☑ Nickel

- ☑ Coping saw
- ☑ Drill
- ☑ ⁷⁄₃₂" (5.5mm), ¼" (6mm), and ³⁄₈" (10mm) drill bits
- ☑ Hammer
- ☑ Thin wire for pulling rubber band

Engineering Advice:

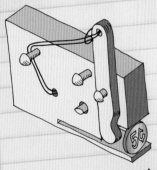

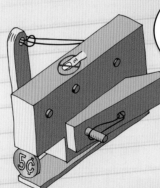

Obviously, I'm not the sharpest tool on the workbench, but I did get this working **safely** and that's what counts.

The coin slot is the only critical dimension in this toy. The nickel needs to fit snugly in the slot. Draw the lines and verify the width using a nickel. Cut the slot a little narrow because you can always sand it wider. If it's too wide, add a little tape.

Ouch! My finger got pinched because I had it on top of the base when I released the hammer. To fix this, I added a dowel to stop the hammer at a 45° angle. I also added a warning to remind myself not to put my finger there.

RICOCHET SHOOTER

A fun puck shooter and a rubber band bouncer combine to create hours of fun. The puck shooter is the brain of the toy. It contains the latch mechanism, the power mechanism, the guide mechanism, and the pusher mechanism. The shooter requires a little bit of sawing, but is worth every minute of it.

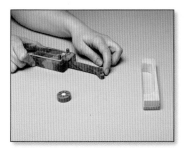
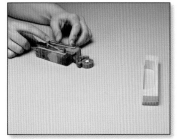

The puck pusher: For accuracy, let's use a fork-shaped pusher that moves in a straight line.

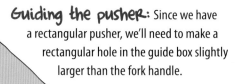

Guiding the pusher: Since we have a rectangular pusher, we'll need to make a rectangular hole in the guide box slightly larger than the fork handle.

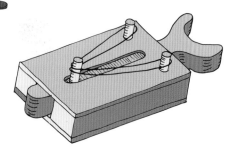

Powering the pusher: To make the shooter compact, we want to make the pusher just a little longer than the guide. However, this prevents us from attaching the rubber band at the back of the pusher. Thus, we will have to attach it to the middle of the pusher by cutting a slot in the guide box and putting a peg into the fork. The peg needs to be toward the back of the pusher to give the maximum travel distance.

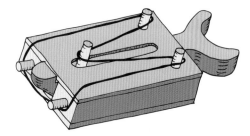

And now, a latch: A notch at the back of the pusher will catch on the top of the guide box to hold the pusher in place. Bevel, or angle, the end of the pusher and stretch the rubber band across the back. The rubber band will lift the latch upward.

Engineering Advice:

When making the pusher, drill hole A first. Then cut the lines in this order: 1, 2, 3, 4.

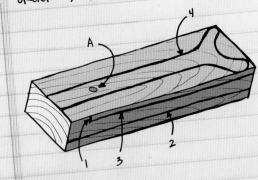

Zany Wooden Toys that **Whiz, Spin, Pop,** and **Fly**

RICOCHET SHOOTER

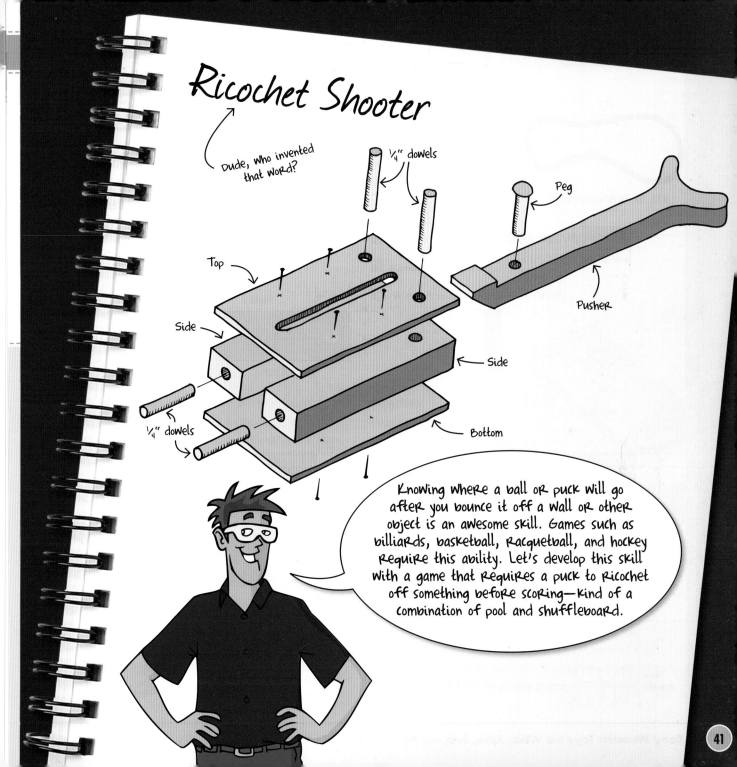

Ricochet Shooter

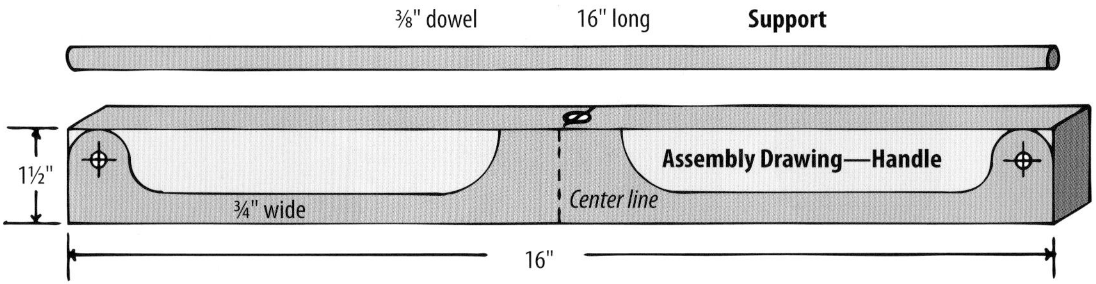
3⁄8" dowel
16" long
Support
Assembly Drawing—Handle
1½"
¾" wide
Center line
16"

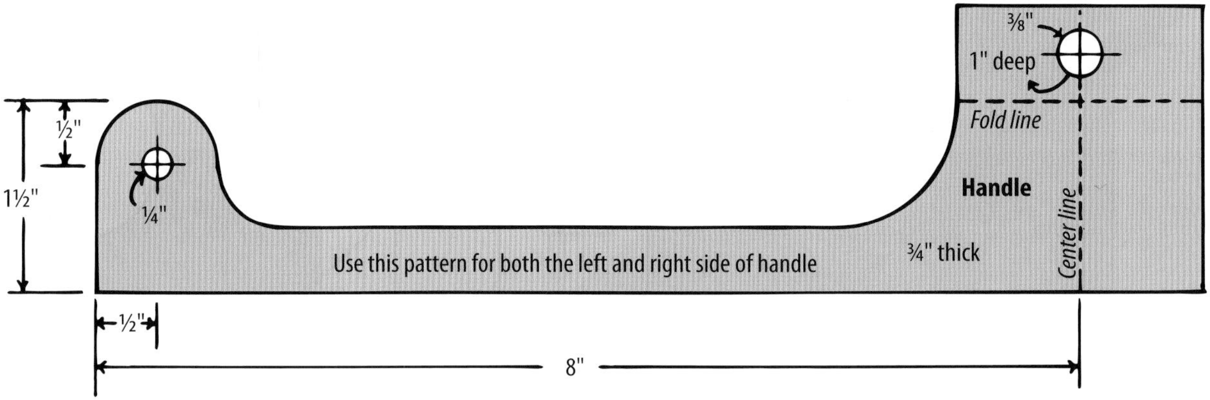
3⁄8"
1" deep
Fold line
½"
1½"
¼"
Handle
Center line
Use this pattern for both the left and right side of handle
¾" thick
½"
8"

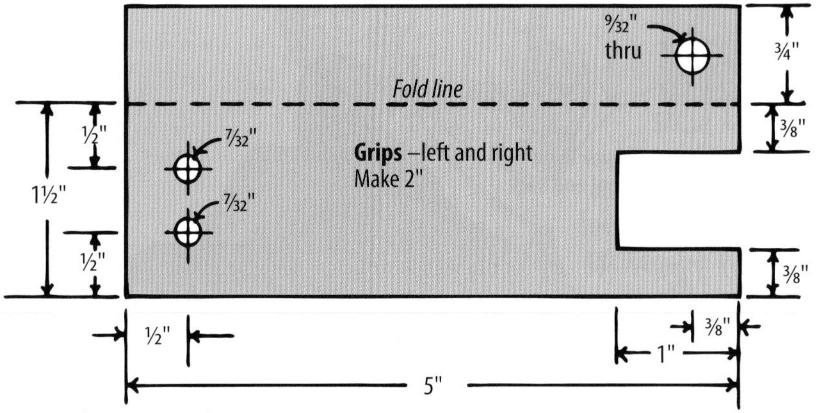
9⁄32"
thru
¾"
Fold line
3⁄8"
½"
7⁄32"
Grips –left and right
Make 2"
1½"
7⁄32"
½"
3⁄8"
½"
3⁄8"
1"
5"

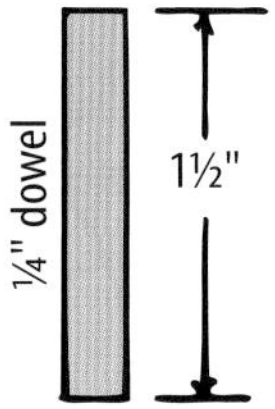
¼" dowel
1½"

Grips – hinge pins
Make 2

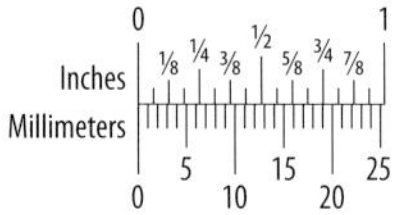
Inches
Millimeters
0
1
⅛ ¼ 3⁄8 ½ 5⁄8 ¾ 7⁄8
5 10 15 20 25

Enlarge pattern 150% for actual size.

Ricochet Shooter

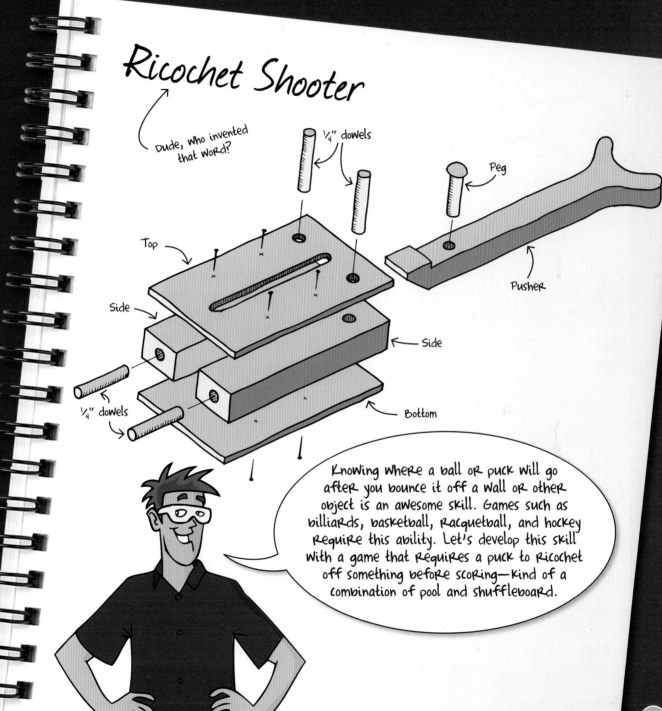

Dude, who invented that word?

¼" dowels

Peg

Top

Side

Side

¼" dowels

Pusher

Bottom

Knowing where a ball or puck will go after you bounce it off a wall or other object is an awesome skill. Games such as billiards, basketball, racquetball, and hockey require this ability. Let's develop this skill with a game that requires a puck to ricochet off something before scoring—kind of a combination of pool and shuffleboard.

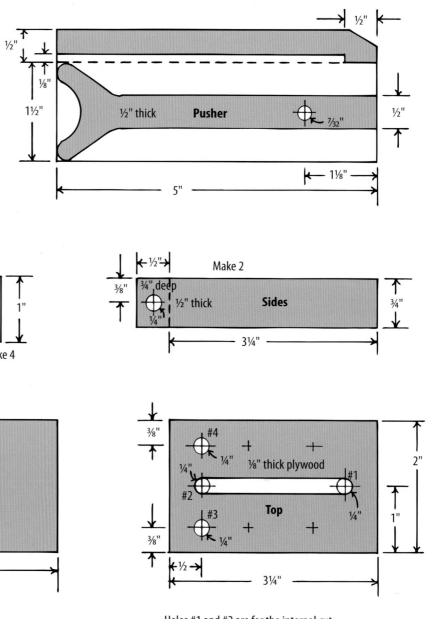

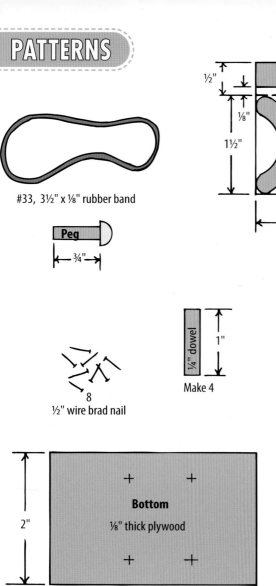

#33, 3½" x ⅛" rubber band

Peg

¾"

½" wire brad nail

8

¼" dowel

Make 4

1"

½" thick **Pusher**

½"

½"

⅛"

1½"

½" thick

7/32"

1⅛"

5"

Make 2

⅜"

½"

¾" deep

½" thick **Sides**

¼"

¾"

3¼"

Bottom

⅛" thick plywood

2"

3¼"

"+" means nail

⅜"

#4

¼"

¼"

⅛" thick plywood

2"

¼"

#2

#1

Top

¼"

⅜"

#3

¼"

1"

½"

3¼"

Holes #1 and #2 are for the internal cut.
Holes #3 and #4 are drilled after assembly
and are ⅝" deep.

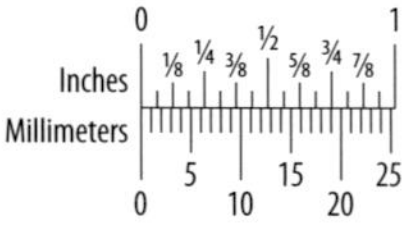

Inches
Millimeters

0   ⅛ ¼ ⅜ ½ ⅝ ¾ ⅞   1

0   5   10   15   20   25

Enlarge pattern 145% for actual size.

Zany Wooden Toys that Whiz, Spin, Pop, and Fly

- ☑ ¾" (19mm) x 1½" (38mm) x 5" (127mm) pine board for pusher
- ☑ ¾" (19mm) x ½" (13mm) x 8" (203mm) pine board for sides of guide box
- ☑ ⅛" (3mm) x 2" (51mm) x 3¼" (83mm) plywood for top and bottom of guide box, 2
- ☑ ¼" (6mm) dowel, 4" (102mm) long for anchor pins
- ☑ Peg
- ☑ ½" (13mm) brads, 8
- ☑ #33, 3½" (89mm) x ⅛" (3mm) rubber band

- ☑ 1" (25mm) dowel for pucks
- ☑ Scrap wood for bouncer
- ☑ ¼" (6mm)-wide rubber bands for bouncer
- ☑ Coping saw
- ☑ Drill
- ☑ 7/32" (5.5mm) and ¼" (6mm) drill bits
- ☑ Hammer
- ☑ Vise for holding pieces while cutting

Game Idea: Bounce the Puck

This is a fun game that uses the ricochet shooter to bounce a puck off a rubber band onto a target. What angles do you need to hit the target? How far away from the bouncer should you be? These questions will be answered as you experiment.

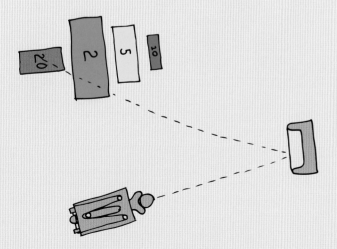

Objective:
Bounce a puck off a rubber band onto a target and get the highest score.

To make the pieces:
Cut ½" (13mm)-wide pieces from a 1" (25mm) dowel for the pucks. Sand them so they'll glide well. For the bouncers, just cut a wide U shape, and then stretch wide rubber bands across the opening.

Setup:
Have a line to shoot behind. Position the bouncer facing the shooting line about 2' (610mm) away. Put pieces of tape marked with different values on the floor. Small pieces of tape should have large values, and large pieces should have small values. Each player gets five pucks and they take turns trying to land on the high-valued tape and knocking their opponents off the tape.

U-Control
SOCCER
PLAYER

This is an easy toy to make, and there are endless games to play with it. Take the time to paint the player with your team's colors or put your own number on it. The soccer ball can be a wooden ball, a rubber bouncy ball, a ping-pong ball, or even a ball made of aluminum foil or masking tape. Gooooal!

*Zany Wooden Toys that **Whiz, Spin, Pop,** and **Fly***

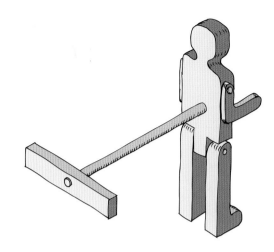

Controlling the player: How to make a little soccer player? Electronics, motors, and remote controls are too complicated. Let's do something like a puppet, but not a hanging puppet like Pinocchio. Instead, let's control our soccer player from behind so we can move it faster and more accurately.

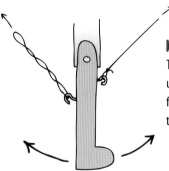

Kicking the ball: To kick the ball, we'll use string to pull the leg forward and a rubber band to pull the leg backward.

Positioning the string: The string on the legs goes straight upward, but it must make a right angle to get back to our hands. To do this, we'll put a hole through the player's body above each leg.

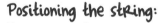

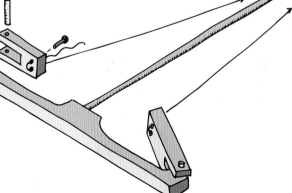

Pulling the string with your fingers would be awkward, so let's make a lever for each leg and hand.

U-Control Soccer Player

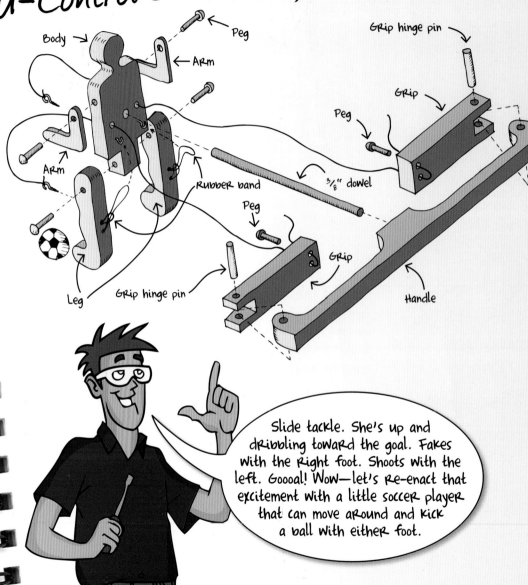

Body

Peg

Arm

Arm

Leg

Rubber band

Peg

Grip hinge pin

Grip hinge pin

Peg

Grip

$^3/_8"$ dowel

Grip hinge pin

Grip

Peg

Grip

Handle

Slide tackle. She's up and dribbling toward the goal. Fakes with the right foot. Shoots with the left. Goooal! Wow—let's re-enact that excitement with a little soccer player that can move around and kick a ball with either foot.

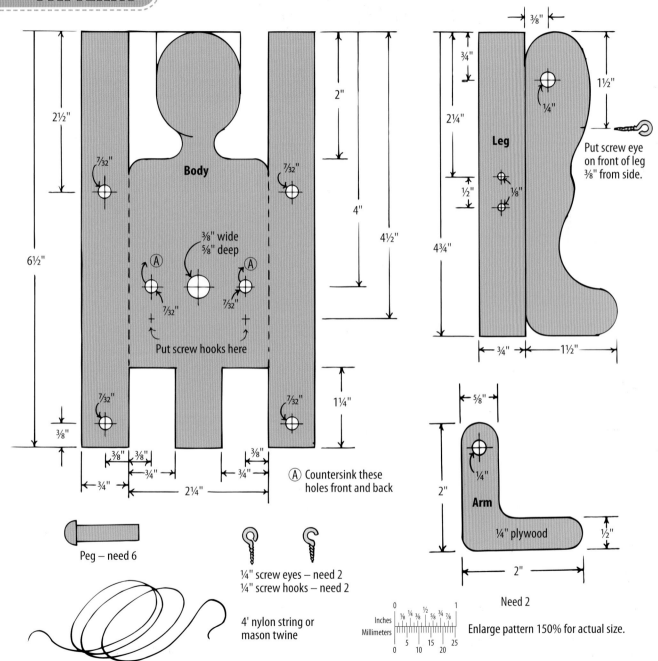

2½"

6½"

7/32"

7/32"

Body

⅜" wide
⅝" deep

Ⓐ

Ⓐ

7/32"

7/32"

Put screw hooks here

7/32"

7/32"

⅜"

⅜" ⅜"

¾"

¾"

¾"

2¼"

2"

4"

4½"

1¼"

Ⓐ Countersink these
holes front and back

⅜"

¾"

¼"

Leg

2¼"

½"

⅛"

4¾"

¾"

1½"

1½"

Put screw eye
on front of leg
⅜" from side.

⅝"

2"

¼"

Arm

¼" plywood

2"

½"

Need 2

Enlarge pattern 150% for actual size.

Peg – need 6

¼" screw eyes – need 2
¼" screw hooks – need 2

4' nylon string or
mason twine

Inches
Millimeters

0   ⅛ ¼ ⅜ ½ ⅝ ¾ ⅞   1

0   5   10   15   20   25

Zany Wooden Toys that Whiz, Spin, Pop, and Fly

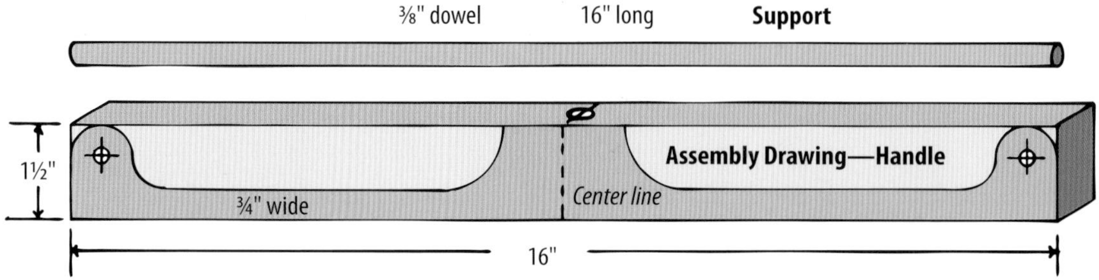
⅜" dowel
16" long
Support
1½"
Assembly Drawing—Handle
¾" wide
Center line
16"

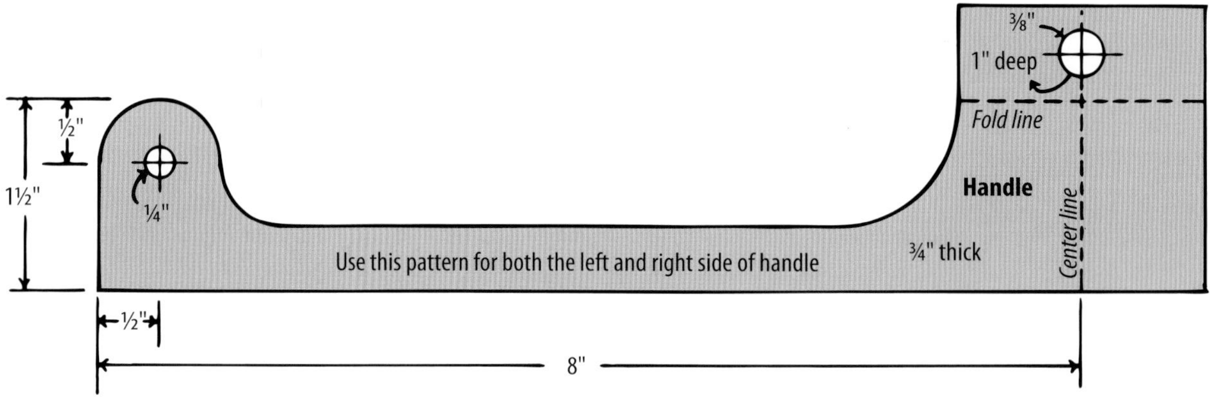
⅜"
1" deep
Fold line
½"
1½"
¼"
Handle
Center line
¾" thick
Use this pattern for both the left and right side of handle
½"
8"

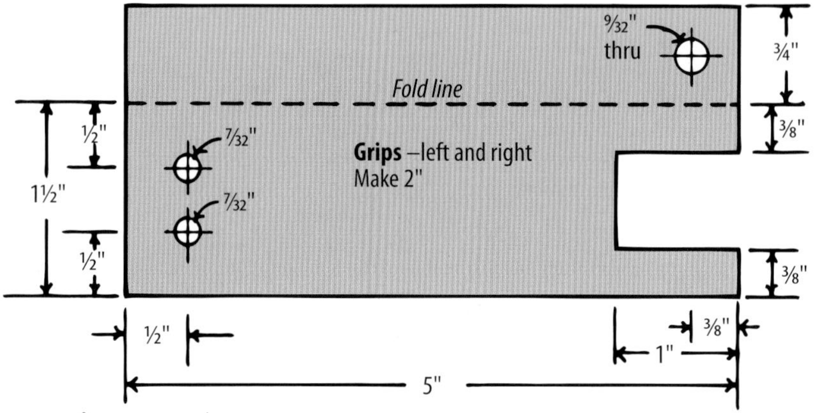
9⁄32"
thru
¾"
Fold line
⅜"
½"
7⁄32"
Grips –left and right
Make 2"
1½"
7⁄32"
½"
⅜"
½"
⅜"
1"
5"

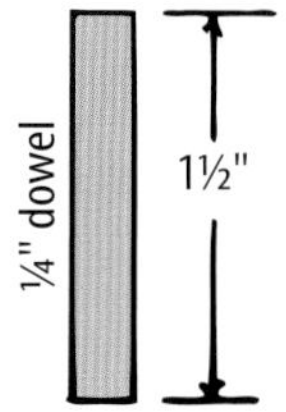
¼" dowel
1½"

Grips – hinge pins
Make 2

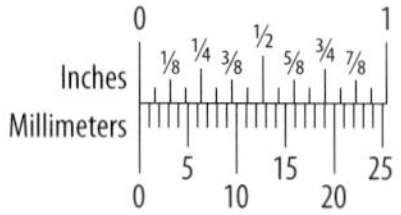
Inches
Millimeters
0
⅛ ¼ ⅜ ½ ⅝ ¾ ⅞
1
5 15 25
0 10 20

Enlarge pattern 150% for actual size.

☑ ¾" (19mm) x 2¼" (57mm) x 6½" (165mm) pine for body

☑ ¾" (19mm) x 1½" (38mm) x 36" (914mm) pine for legs, handle, and grips

☑ ¼" (6mm) x 2" (51mm) x 4" (102mm) plywood for arms

☑ ⅜" (10mm) dowel, 16" (406mm) long for support

☑ ¼" (6mm) dowel, 3" (76mm) long for grip hinge pins

☑ Pegs, 6

☑ ¼" (6mm) hook screws, 2

☑ ¼" (6mm) eye screws, 2

☑ 4' (1,219mm) nylon string or mason twine

☑ Rubber bands, 2

☑ A small ball of some type

☑ Coping saw

☑ Drill

☑ ⅛" (3mm), ⁷⁄₃₂" (5.5mm), ¼" (6mm), ⁹⁄₃₂" (7mm), and ⅜" (10mm) drill bits

☑ Awl to make starter holes

☑ Vise for holding pieces while cutting

☑ Needle-nose pliers to screw in hook screws and eye screws. (Don't even think about using your teeth!)

Engineering Advice:

1: You need to adjust the string so the leg is straight down when your hand is halfway between being opened and closed. Rather than tying knots, use a peg to hold the string—it's easier to adjust.

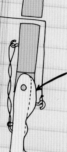

2: A straight leg requires a lot of force. I added a large "muscle" to the leg so the string has more leverage.

3: You don't need to glue the dowel into the back of the soccer player. The loose dowel allows your player to kick sideways, dive, and slide tackle.

4: Loop the rubber band through the leg to save on eye screws.

LAUNCHERS

This chapter will teach you how to make toys that flip, flick, shoot, and fire objects through the air. The first project is the quick and easy Tissue Launching Crossbow (page 53). Follow the step-by-step instructions, and you'll be ready to pass the tissues to your favorite sick person from a healthy distance. Also included are the Ping-Pong Ball Launcher (page 65), Rapid-Fire Nickel Launcher (page 70), Quarter Flipper (page 76), and Gold Medal Backflip Skier (page 81).

Tissue-Launching
CROSSBOW

This crossbow is a hygienic and quick way to deliver a tissue to someone with a cold. The next time someone asks you for a tissue, duck into the workshop and whip up one of these. You'll build it so quickly your ailing friend won't even notice the delay. Simple, straight cuts and a few holes, and you'll be launching tissues with amazing accuracy in no time.

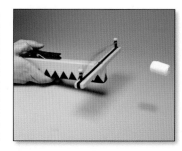

Aerodynamic tissues:
Have you ever tried to throw a tissue? It's impossible. The tissue only goes a couple of feet. We'll have to make the tissue more aerodynamic. Fold a tissue until it is 1" (25mm) wide (1), roll it into a cylinder (2), and tape once around the roll to hold its shape (3).

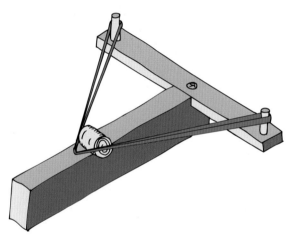

Launching the tissue:
To send the tissue, let's use something like a slingshot, but mount the handle horizontally. Then we can put on a latch that will allow us to load and aim the tissue.

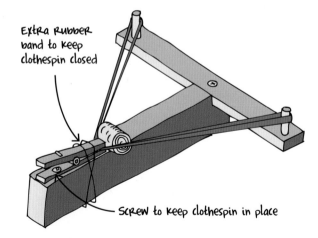

Extra rubber band to keep clothespin closed

Screw to keep clothespin in place

Making the latch:
To form the latch, we'll attach a clothespin to the handle. The grip of the clothespin will hold the rubber band while the tissue roll is being loaded.

*Zany Wooden Toys that **Whiz, Spin, Pop,** and **Fly***

Tissue-Launching Crossbow

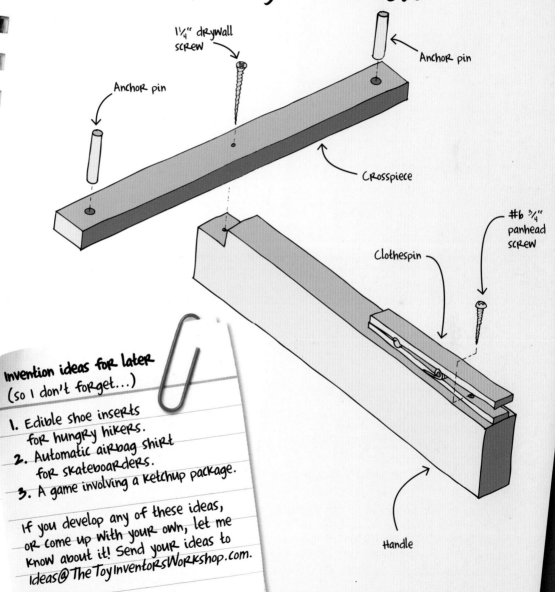

1¼" drywall screw

Anchor pin

Anchor pin

Crosspiece

#6 ¾" panhead screw

Clothespin

Handle

Invention ideas for later
(so I don't forget...)

1. Edible shoe inserts for hungry hikers.
2. Automatic airbag shirt for skateboarders.
3. A game involving a ketchup package.

If you develop any of these ideas, or come up with your own, let me know about it! Send your ideas to Ideas@TheToyInventorsWorkshop.com.

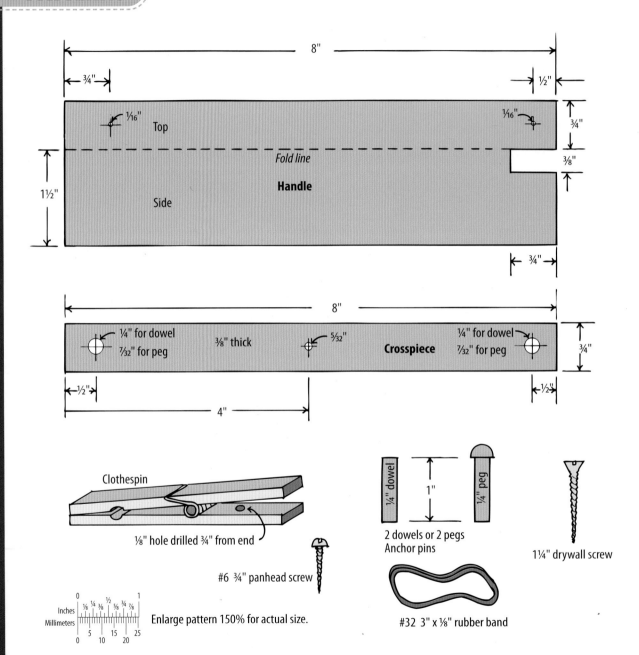

8"

¾"   ½"

1/16"   Top   1/16"   ¾"

Fold line   3/8"

1½"   **Handle**

Side

¾"

8"

¼" for dowel   3/8" thick   5/32"   **Crosspiece**   ¼" for dowel   ¾"

7/32" for peg   7/32" for peg

½"   ½"

4"

Clothespin

⅛" hole drilled ¾" from end

#6 ¾" panhead screw

¼" dowel   1"   ¼" peg

2 dowels or 2 pegs
Anchor pins

1¼" drywall screw

#32 3" x ⅛" rubber band

Inches   0   ⅛ ¼ ⅜ ½ ⅝ ¾ ⅞   1
Millimeters   0   5   10   15   20   25

Enlarge pattern 150% for actual size.

TISSUE-LAUNCHING CROSSBOW STEP-BY-STEP

- ☑ ¾" (19mm) x 1½" (38mm) x 8" (203mm) pine board for handle
- ☑ ⅜" (10mm) x ¾" (19mm) x 8" (203mm) pine board for crosspiece
- ☑ Pegs or pieces of 1" (25mm)-long ¼" (6mm) dowel, 2
- ☑ Clothespin (metal spring-type)
- ☑ #6 x ¾" (19mm) panhead screw
- ☑ 1¼" (32mm) drywall screw
- ☑ #32, 3" x ⅛" (3mm) rubber bands, 2
- ☑ Facial tissues
- ☑ Coping saw
- ☑ Drill
- ☑ 1/16" (1.5mm), ⅛" (3mm), 5/32" (4mm), and 7/32" (5.5mm) drill bits
- ☑ Hammer
- ☑ Awl to make starter holes
- ☑ Screwdriver to match screw
- ☑ Vise
- ☑ Ruler
- ☑ Square
- ☑ Pencil
- ☑ Invisible tape
- ☑ Masking Tape

Engineering Advice:

You may need to use an extra rubber band to help keep the clothespin closed.

Place the tissue-launching rubber band ¼" (6mm) to ½" (13mm) up on the pegs. If it's at the base of the pegs, the rubber band will go under the tissue roll and simply pop it into the air. Of course, this is a useful piece of information to keep in mind when someone wants to borrow your crossbow...sort of a safety (or booby-trap!) switch for your toy.

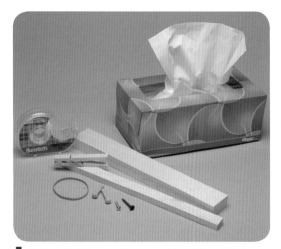

1 Collect all of the supplies on the Materials and Tools List. If you don't have wooden pegs for the anchor pins, use pieces of a ¼" (6mm) dowel. Just use a ¼" (6mm) drill bit when it comes time to drill the holes.

2 Use the ruler to measure a length of 8" (203mm) from the end of the ¾" (19mm) x 1½" (38mm) board. This will be the handle. Make a small pencil mark at 8" (203mm) on the wide surface of the board. Always make your marks parallel to the lines on the ruler.

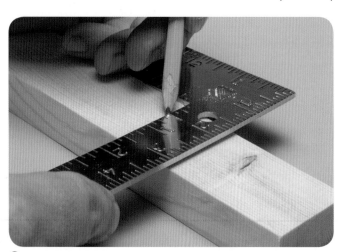

3 Use the square to draw a straight line across the board at your pencil mark. Make sure you keep one leg of the square pressed firmly against the side of the board. This ensures your line is perpendicular to the edge. Put an X on the far side of the line to remind yourself where to place the saw.

4 Mark the depth of the notch on the handle. Start by making a mark on the line you just drew ⅜" (10mm) from the edge. Move the square about 2" (51mm) down the handle and make another mark on the handle ⅜" (10mm) from the side. Align one edge of the square on these marks and draw a line about 2" (51mm) long.

Zany Wooden Toys that Whiz, Spin, Pop, and Fly

5 Mark the back of the notch by measuring ¾" (19mm) in from your first line. Use the square to make a straight line perpendicular to the edge at your mark. Remember to hold the square firmly against the side of the board.

6 Turn the board on its edge. Use the square to mark the board length and the back of the notch on the side. The marks will help you align your saw.

7 Measure and mark an 8" (203mm) length of the ⅜" (10mm) x ¾" (19mm) board (similar to Steps 2 and 3).

The crosspiece can be cut from another piece of ¾" (19mm) x 1½" (38mm) x 8" (203mm) wood. Just mark the ⅜" (10mm) width, mount the wood in a vise, and saw down the line. You may have to rotate the blade on your coping saw to make the cut.

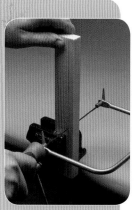

8 Using the square, mark the locations for both of the $7/32$" (5.5mm) peg holes in the crosspiece. Each hole requires two measurements: one from the end and one from the side. For each hole, measure in $1/2$" (13mm) from the end, and put a small pencil mark there. Next, move the square to the side and draw a line perpendicular to the edge, through your first mark. Finally, with the square still in place, mark $3/8$" (10mm) in from the side.

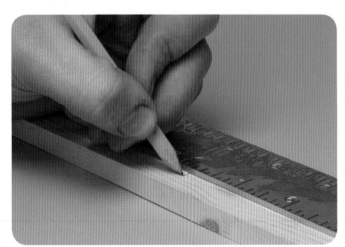

9 Mark the location for the center hole by measuring in 4" (102mm) from either end and $3/8$" (10mm) from the side. This intersection marks the $5/32$" (4mm) hole for the drywall screw.

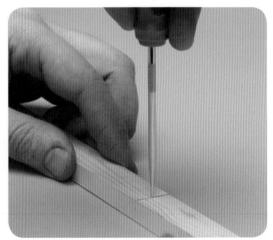

10 Use the awl to make a small indentation at the locations of the three holes. This will help prevent the drill bit from wandering.

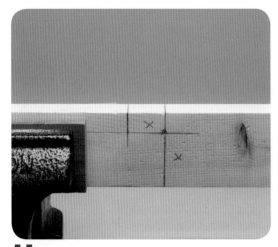

11 Mount the handle horizontally in the vise, with the end line positioned outside the vise.

12 Place the coping saw on the waste side of the line, and cut off the piece of wood you do not need.

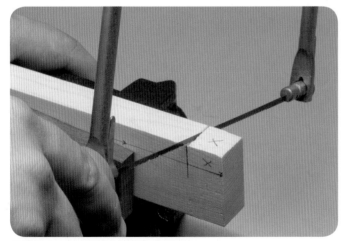

13 Move the saw to the line at the back of the notch and make the ⅜" (10mm)-deep cut. Keep the teeth of the saw parallel to the top edge of the board so that the cut is ⅜" (10mm) deep on the front and the back.

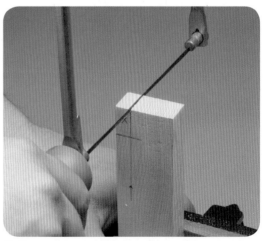

14 Reposition the handle vertically in the vise. Use the square to mark the bottom of the notch on the end of the board and saw down the line to complete the notch.

*Zany Wooden Toys that **Whiz, Spin, Pop, and Fly***

15 Cut off the 8" (203mm) board for the crosspiece.

16 Place the ⅜" (10mm) x ¾" (19mm) x 8" (203mm) crosspiece on some scrap wood. Drill the ⁷⁄₃₂" (5.5mm) holes in the ends for the pegs and the ⁵⁄₃₂" (4mm) hole in the middle for the drywall screw.

17 Twist the top and bottom blades of the clothespin so you can drill the ⅛" (3mm) hole at the back. It should be about ½" (13mm) from the end. (You can just guess this dimension.) Put the clothespin on a piece of scrap wood and drill the ⅛" (3mm) hole.

18 Pound the two pegs into the ends of the crosspiece. The pegs should extend about ⅛" (3mm) on the bottom of the crosspiece.

19 Put the crosspiece in the notch of the handle, with the pegs' heads upward. Align the center hole in the crosspiece with the center of the handle. (You can eyeball, or estimate, this.) Insert the drywall screw in the crosspiece and push down hard. This should leave a mark in the notch of the handle.

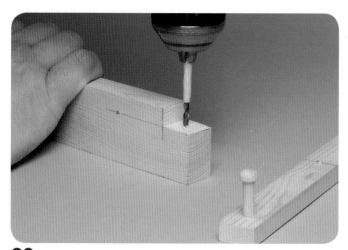

20 Remove the crosspiece and drill a ⅛" (3mm) hole about ¾" (19mm) deep in the handle. Mark the depth on the drill bit using a piece of masking tape.

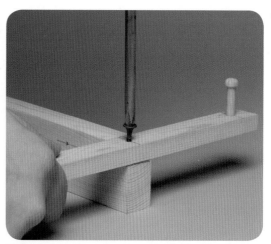

21 Insert the 1¼" (32mm) drywall screw into the hole in the crosspiece and then screw it into the handle.

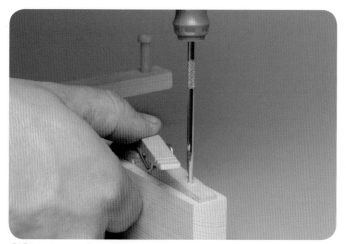

22 Align the clothespin with the back of the handle and centered between the sides. Push the awl through the hole in the clothespin and into the handle to mark the screw location.

23 Insert the screw through the clothespin and into the handle. Twist the clothespin back into position.

24 Double- or triple-up one of the rubber bands over the front of the clothespin. This will help the clothespin stay closed.

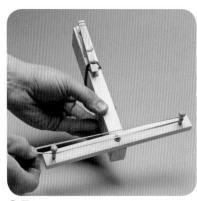

25 Stretch the other rubber band between the two pegs in the crosspiece. Keep it near the top of the pegs.

26 Fold a facial tissue into a 1" (25mm)-wide strip. Roll it loosely into a ¾" (19mm)-diameter column. Put a 2" (51mm) piece of invisible tape around it to hold its shape. See the drawings on page 54 for further instruction.

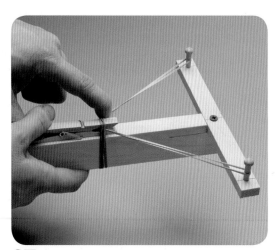

27 Open the clothespin, and pull both sides of the rubber band into its jaws. Close the clothespin to hold the rubber band.

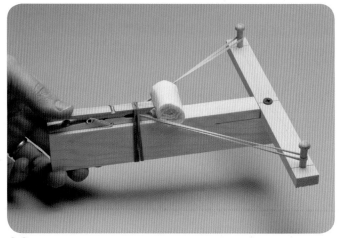

28 Insert the rolled-up tissue sideways between the sides of the rubber band. Aim, and push down on the clothespin to release the tissue. You have successfully delivered your first tissue!

Ping-Pong
BALL
LAUNCHER

The main mechanism on this toy is an easy-to-make latch that relies on the fact that wood can bend and is rather springy when it is cut thin. The thin piece of wood on the handle acts as both the spring for the latch and the trigger. You can adjust the springiness of the wood by sanding it thinner. Have fun launching ping-pong balls when you're done experimenting!

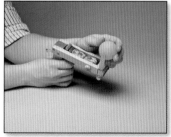

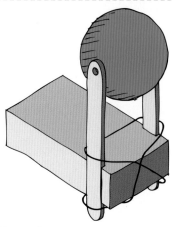

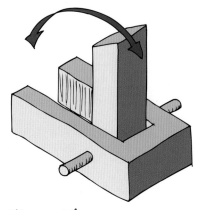

The platform: A ping-pong ball is about 1½" (38mm) in diameter—about the same width as a 1" (25mm) x 2" (51mm) board. It doesn't take much strength to hold a ping-pong ball. Let's pinch it between two craft sticks. The craft sticks can be held to the board using rubber bands.

The paddle: Instead of my finger, a little wooden smacker can fly up and hit the ball. This will be powered by a rubber band.

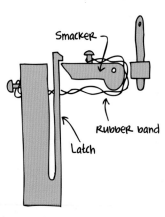

Smacker

Rubber band

Latch

The latch: Because the paddle will be rotating upward toward the ball, I can add a latch to hold it back. As the paddle comes down into the ready position, it presses the latch backward until it slips into the notch and locks the paddle in place. Pulling the latch backward will release the paddle.

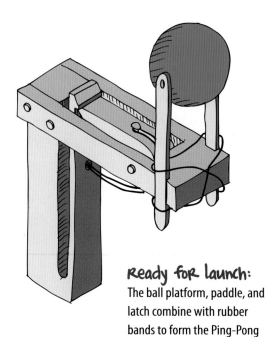

Ready for launch: The ball platform, paddle, and latch combine with rubber bands to form the Ping-Pong Ball Launcher.

PING-PONG BALL LAUNCHER

Ping-Pong Ball Launcher

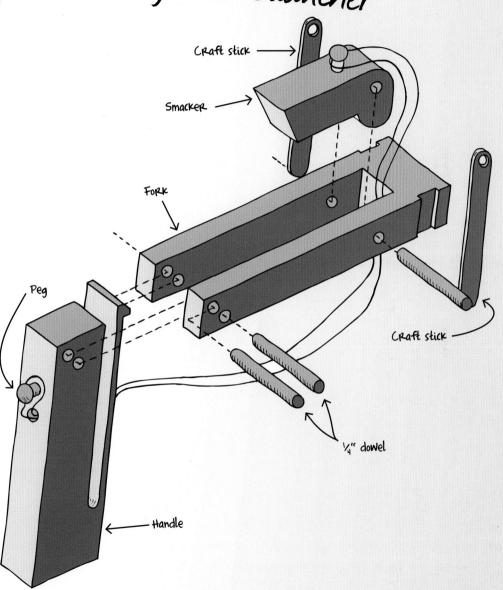

Craft stick

Smacker

Fork

Peg

Craft stick

$\frac{1}{4}$" dowel

Handle

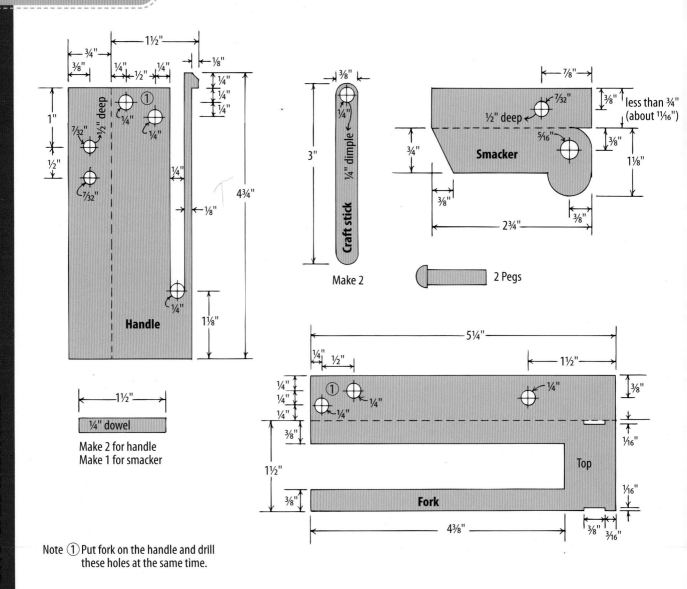

Craft stick
Make 2

¼" dimple

Smacker

2 Pegs

Handle

¼" dowel

Make 2 for handle
Make 1 for smacker

Top

Fork

Note ① Put fork on the handle and drill these holes at the same time.

Inches
Millimeters

Enlarge pattern 160% for actual size.

MATERIALS & TOOLS

- ☑ ³/₄" (19mm) x 1½" (38mm) x 13" (330mm) for fork, smacker, and handle
- ☑ ¼" (6mm) dowel, 4½" (114mm) long
- ☑ Pegs, 2
- ☑ Craft sticks, 2
- ☑ #64, 3½" (89mm) x ¼" (6mm) rubber band
- ☑ Ping-Pong balls
- ☑ Coping saw
- ☑ Drill
- ☑ ⁷/₃₂" (5.5mm), ¼" (6mm), ⁵/₁₆" (8mm) drill bits
- ☑ Fine sandpaper for smoothing the latch

Engineering Advice:

Align the fork with the handle and then drill the two ¼" (6mm) holes to connect these parts. This will result in perfect alignment of the holes.

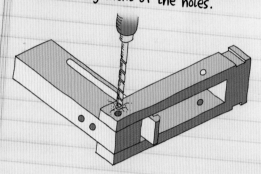

One day, after finishing a game of ping-pong, I picked up the ball and, for some unknown reason, gave it a flick. It flew! I was amazed at how little effort it took to launch the ball across the room. Now we've got a little contraption to launch ping-pong balls using the same action.

Rapid-Fire
NICKEL LAUNCHER

Turn the knob, and a nickel is launched with a loud "Bang!" Turn the knob faster, and nickels continue to fly out almost faster than you can see them. This toy does require gluing and clamping three pieces together, so there's a little delay halfway through the project. Get the glue drying while you work on the other components, and everything should finish up at about the same time. The grooves on the bottom are easily done on a table saw, but a hand saw or miter saw will also do the trick.

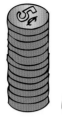

The pucks: We want to shoot pucks and the more the better. Thus, they must be fairly thin (⅛" [3mm] or so) so we can stack a whole bunch of them. Nickels are about the right size and only cost about 5¢. Some stores will even have them on sale—20 for a buck. Let's use nickels.

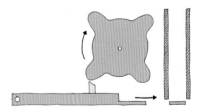

Launching the pucks: We'll need a thin piece of wood that will push out the bottom nickel without hitting the one above it. Let's call this piece the rammer.

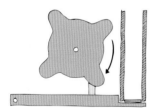
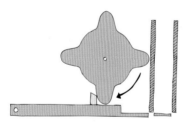

How to shoot out puck after puck: Now that's a tough one. Something needs to push the rammer backward and then release it. A star gear can do this, but it has to be the right size. I built a little model so I could measure and adjust pieces.

*Zany Wooden Toys that **Whiz, Spin, Pop, and Fly***

Rapid-Fire Nickel Launcher

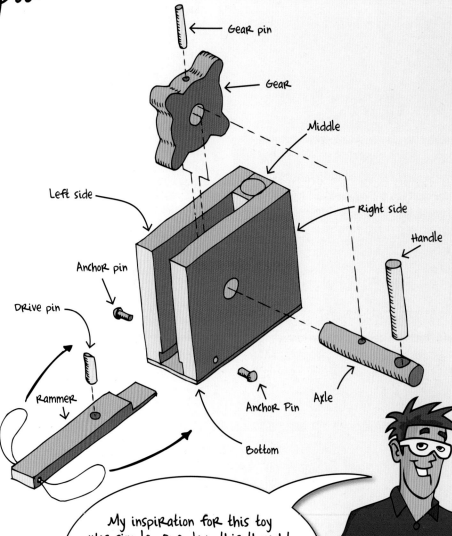

PATTERNS

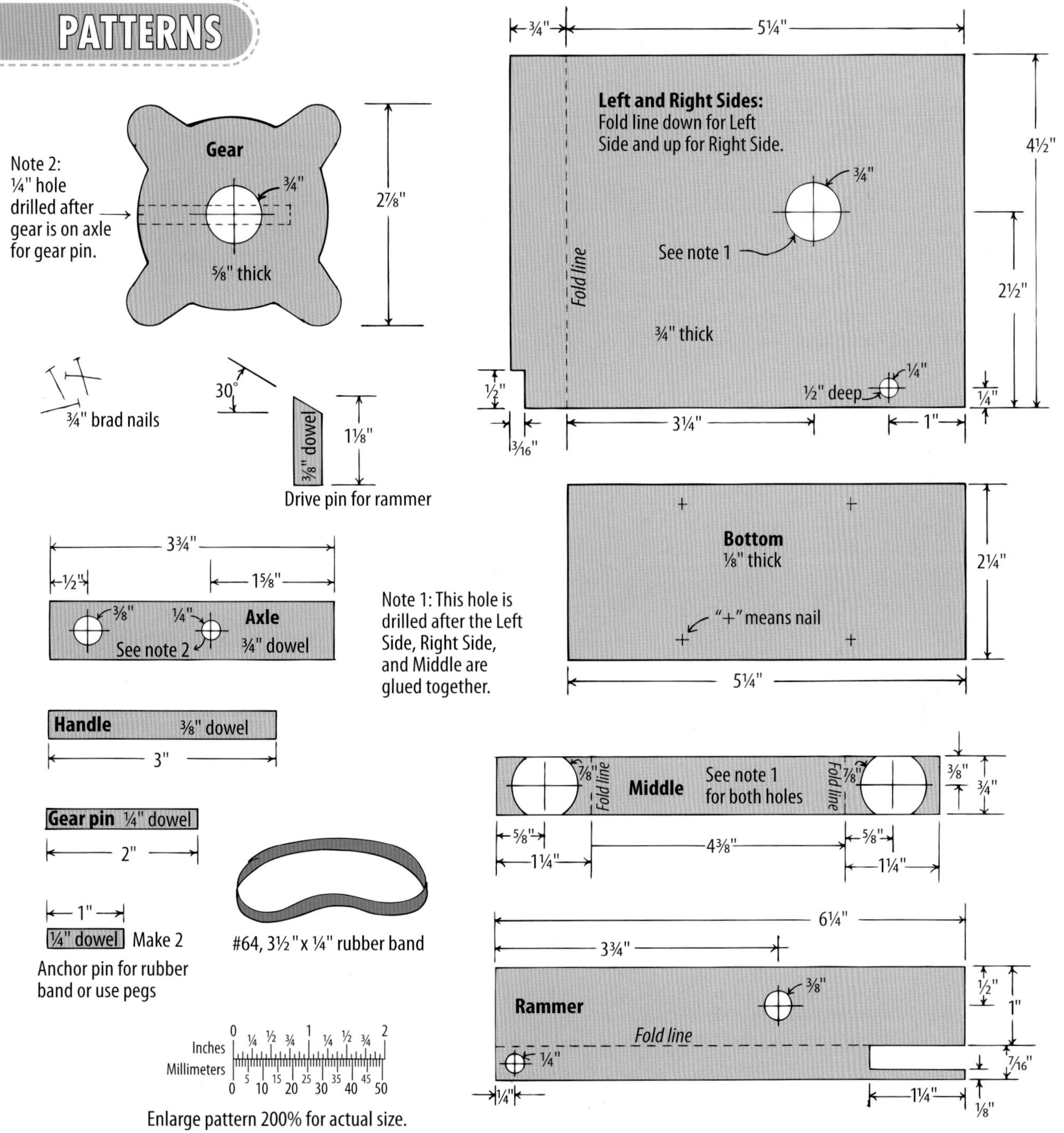

Gear
Note 2: ¼" hole drilled after gear is on axle for gear pin.
¾"
⅝" thick
2⅞"
¾" brad nails
30°
⅜" dowel
1⅛"
Drive pin for rammer
3¾"
½"
1⅝"
⅜"
¼"
Axle
See note 2
¾" dowel
Note 1: This hole is drilled after the Left Side, Right Side, and Middle are glued together.
Handle ⅜" dowel
3"
Gear pin ¼" dowel
2"
1"
¼" dowel Make 2
Anchor pin for rubber band or use pegs
#64, 3½" x ¼" rubber band
Inches 0 ¼ ½ ¾ 1 ¼ ½ ¾ 2
Millimeters 0 5 10 15 20 25 30 35 40 45 50
¾"
5¼"
Left and Right Sides:
Fold line down for Left Side and up for Right Side.
¾"
4½"
See note 1
Fold line
2½"
¾" thick
½"
¼"
½" deep
¼"
3⁄16"
3¼"
1"
Bottom
⅛" thick
"+" means nail
2¼"
5¼"
⅞"
Fold line
Middle
See note 1 for both holes
Fold line
⅞"
⅜"
¾"
⅝"
1¼"
4⅜"
⅝"
1¼"
6¼"
3¾"
⅜"
Rammer
Fold line
¼"
½"
1"
7⁄16"
¼"
1¼"
⅛"

Enlarge pattern 200% for actual size.

1 Cut out the left side, right side, and middle. Make the rabbets on the sidepieces. Do not drill any holes.

2 Use a pencil or awl to mark the location for the ⅞" (22mm) hole on the top and bottom of the middle piece.

3 Glue and clamp the left side, middle, and right side together. The tops and fronts should be flush with each other. The middle is about a nickel's width shorter than the sides.

4 Drill the ⅞" (22mm) hole after the glue has dried. Drill this hole about halfway deep from the top and then finish off the hole from the bottom.

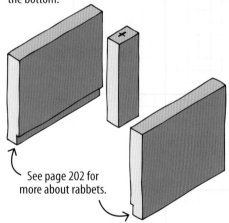

See page 202 for more about rabbets.

5 Put a ¾" (19mm) piece of scrap wood between the sides for support and then drill the 1" (25mm) hole for the axle. Drill the ¼" (6mm) holes for the anchor pins to hold the rubber band.

6 Attach the bottom with the ¾" (19mm) wire nails.

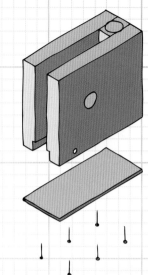

7 Cut out the gear and sand it to ⅝" (16mm) thick.

8 Put the gear on the axle and then drill the ¼" (6mm) hole for the gear pin. Put a mark on the gear and the handle to help align the holes later.

9 Assemble as shown in the exploded diagram.

Rabbits? I don't see no stinkin' Rabbits. See page 202.

- ☑ ³/₄" (19mm) x 4½" (114mm) x 5¼" (133mm) pine boards for sides, 2

- ☑ ³/₄" (19mm) x 3" (76mm) x 3" (76mm) pine board for gear [this needs to be sanded to ⅝" (16mm) thick]

- ☑ ³/₄" (19mm) x 1¼" (32mm) x 4⅜" (111mm) pine board for middle

- ☑ ⅛" (3mm) x 2¼" (57mm) x 5¼" (133mm) pine board for bottom

- ☑ ⁷/₁₆" (11mm) x 1" (25mm) x 6¼" (159mm) hardwood, such as oak or maple, for rammer

- ☑ ³/₄" (19mm) dowel, 3¾" (95mm) long for axle

- ☑ ⅜" (10mm) dowel, 5" (127mm) long for handle and drive pin

- ☑ ¼" (6mm) dowel, 2" (51mm) long for gear pin

- ☑ Pegs or 1" (25mm) pieces of ¼" (6mm) dowel, 2

- ☑ ³/₄" (19mm) wire nails with heads for bottom, 6

- ☑ #64, 3½" (89mm) x ¼" (6mm) rubber band

- ☑ White or yellow glue

- ☑ Nickels galore

- ☑ Handsaw, miter saw and miter box, or table saw

- ☑ Coping saw

- ☑ Drill

- ☑ ⁷/₃₂" (5.5mm), ¼" (6mm), ⅜" (10mm), ⅞" (22mm), ³/₄" (19mm) drill bits

- ☑ Hammer

- ☑ Clamps with 3" (76mm) opening

- ☑ Vise for holding pieces

- ☑ Sandpaper for smoothing gear

Engineering Advice:

Make the rammer from hardwood, such as oak, maple, or ebony (just kidding about the last one—it's way too expensive). If you use softwood, such as pine, the end of the rammer will splinter after launching a few hundred nickels.

To keep the knob turning smoothly, sand all the surfaces that rub against each other, using 220-grit sandpaper. Then lubricate the surfaces with graphite by rubbing a pencil over them until they are solid gray.

QUARTER FLIPPER

If you ever need to make a decision, settle a dispute, or start the backyard Super Bowl, then you'll want to make the Quarter Flipper. Sure, you can flip a coin with your thumb, but this gadget will flip a quarter so fast you can hear it spin. The two-step cocking action and the release latch are easy to make and add to the mechanical fun of this toy.

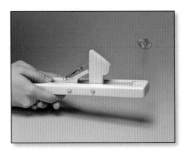

Zany Wooden Toys that Whiz, Spin, Pop, and Fly

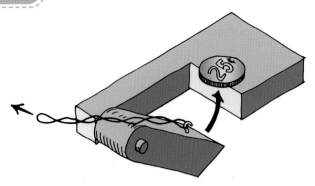

Holding the coin: The quarter must be positioned on the flipper so it hangs over an edge.

Flipping the coin: Something has to fly up and hit the edge of the coin. A little paddle rotating on a dowel could be positioned to hit the very edge of the coin. We'll use a rubber band to swing the paddle.

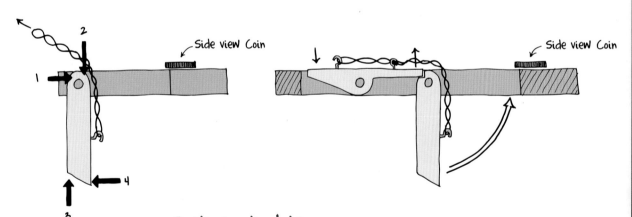

Positioning the latch: The rubber band wants to pull the paddle counterclockwise. Thus, our latch must apply an opposite force in the clockwise direction. We could put the latch at any of the four arrows shown in the drawing. A latch at arrows 2, 3, or 4 would require adding some contraption above or below the handle. Instead, let's put the latch at arrow 1, by putting a notch in the paddle and using a little seesaw to hold the paddle in place. The rubber band will hold the latch in place.

Quarter Flipper

Rubber band is folded in half for more power

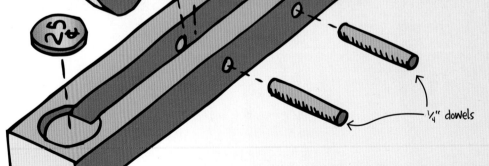

Latch

Paddle

Handle

¼" dowels

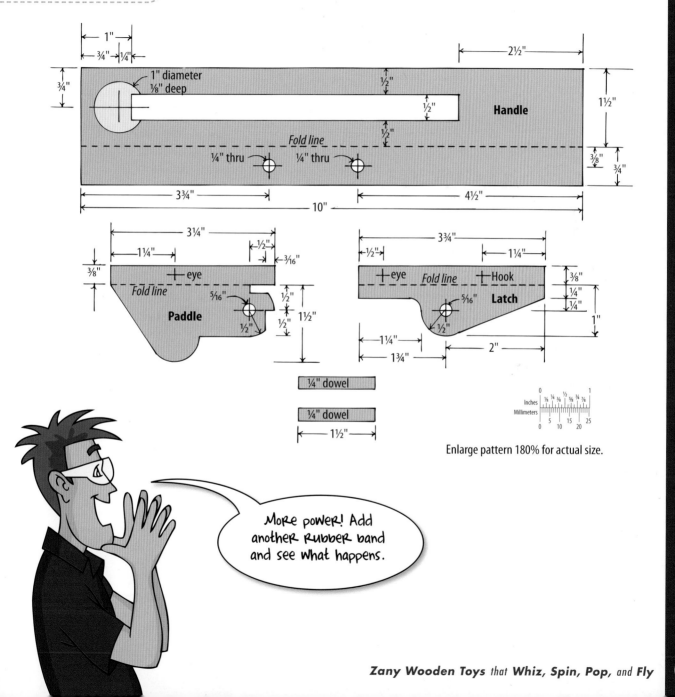

1"
¾" ¼"
¾"
1" diameter
⅛" deep
2½"
½"
½"
Handle
1½"
Fold line
½"
⅜"
¾"
¼" thru   ¼" thru
3¾"
4½"
10"

3¼"
1¼"
½"
³⁄₁₆"
⅜"
+ eye
Fold line
½"
⁵⁄₁₆"
1½"
Paddle
½"   ½"

3¾"
½"
1¼"
+ eye   Fold line   + Hook
⅜"
¼"
¼"
⁵⁄₁₆"   Latch
½"
1"
1¼"
2"
1¾"

¼" dowel

¼" dowel
1½"

Inches
Millimeters

Enlarge pattern 180% for actual size.

MoRe poweR! Add another Rubber band and see what happens.

- ☑ ¾" (19mm) x 1½" (38mm) x 10" (254mm) pine board for handle
- ☑ ⅜" (10mm) x 1½" (38mm) x 7" (178mm) for paddle and latch
- ☑ ¼" (6mm) dowel 3" (76mm) long
- ☑ ½" (13mm) eye screws, 3
- ☑ #64, 3½" (89mm) x ¼" (6mm) rubber band
- ☑ Quarter
- ☑ Decision to be made
- ☑ Coping saw
- ☑ Drill
- ☑ ¼" (6mm), ⁵⁄₁₆" (8mm), and 1" (25mm) drill bits
- ☑ Awl to mark starter holes
- ☑ Needle-nose pliers to screw in eye screw

Engineering Advice:

To make it easier to get the paddle into the cocked position, I added the second notch in the paddle to hold it in the half-cocked position and a handle so the paddle can be grabbed from below.

Drill a shallow 1" (25mm)-diameter hole to keep the quarter in position.

What if a bionic man flipped a quarter with his thumb? Now we know!

Gold Medal
BACKFLIP SKIER

"Duuude, gnarly wipe-out! Total yard sale." Okay, your skier probably won't stick the landing the first time through the terrain park, but better him than you. You'll need a little 1" (25mm) hinge for this project, but that's the most difficult part about it. Make the skis out of a paint stick, wooden ruler, fruit crate, or whatever you have. Much of the fun is dressing the skier with the season's latest fashion. Once he masters the backflip, take him to the lodge and paint him a respectable outfit.

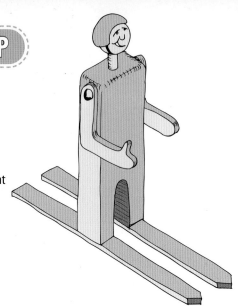

Making the skier: The skier is made of two skis, two arms, two legs, one head (with helmet, of course), and one body. I don't think we need to invent anything here. Perhaps a body cast later?

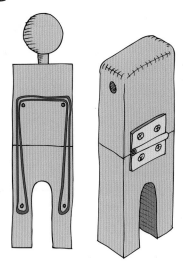

Adding the hinge: The skier needs to bend at the waist, but only in the forward direction, not in the backward direction. We could make a hinge out of wood, as we did in Thumb-Action Marble Shooter (page 24), but that might be a little bulky for our skier-dude. Let's use a little metal hinge. It will be lighter and faster. A rubber band will be the back muscle.

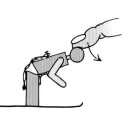

Perfecting the flip: If the skier stands perfectly straight, then the flipping action will just make him tumble backwards. We need to make sure that he's always leaning a little forward so the flipping action pops him into the air a little. To do this, we'll cut the waist at an angle.

PATTERNS

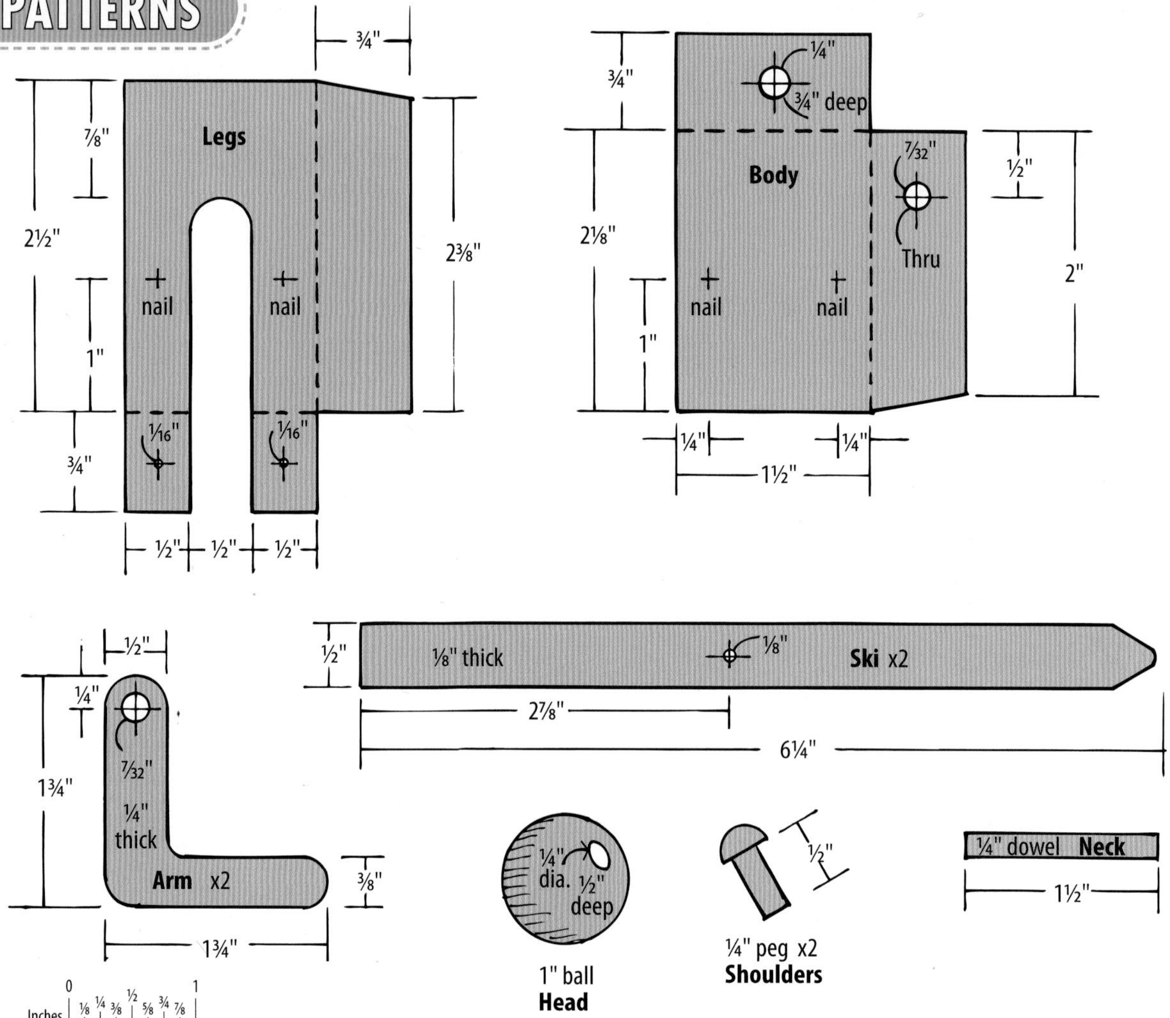

Legs
nail
nail
⅞"
2½"
1"
¾"
¾"
2⅜"
1⁄16"
1⁄16"
½"
½"
½"
Body
¼"
¾" deep
7⁄32"
Thru
nail
nail
¾"
2⅛"
1"
½"
2"
¼"
¼"
1½"
⅛" thick
⅛"
Ski x2
½"
2⅞"
6¼"
½"
¼"
1¾"
7⁄32"
¼" thick
Arm x2
⅜"
1¾"
¼" dia.
½" deep
1" ball
Head
½"
¼" peg x2
Shoulders
¼" dowel Neck
1½"

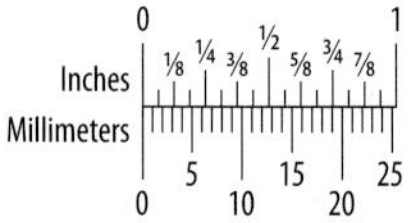

Inches
Millimeters
0
⅛
¼
⅜
½
⅝
¾
⅞
1
5
10
15
20
25

Enlarge pattern 145% for actual size.

This toy is fascinating because of the many properties of physics demonstrated during a simple flip: equal and opposite forces, center of gravity, momentum, kinetic energy, and many more. The average student will be halfway through college before he or she understands all of the math involved. But this toy provides the direct, hands-on experience needed for the concepts to make sense in a freshman college physics course and students should consider this project a prerequisite.

MATERIALS & TOOLS

- ☑ ¾" (19mm) x 1½" (38mm) x 5" (127mm) pine board for body and legs
- ☑ ¼" (6mm) x 2" (51mm) x 4" (102mm) plywood or pine for arms
- ☑ ⅛" (3mm) x ½" (13mm) x 13" (330mm) pine board or plywood for skis
- ☑ ¼" (6mm) dowel, 1½" (38mm) long for neck
- ☑ Pegs for shoulders, 2
- ☑ 1" (25mm) wooden ball for head
- ☑ 1" (25mm) metal hinge, with screws, for waist
- ☑ #4 x ½" (13mm) flathead screws for skis, 2
- ☑ ¾" (19mm) wire nails with heads, 4
- ☑ #32, 3" (76mm) x ⅛" (3mm) rubber band
- ☑ Coping saw
- ☑ Drill
- ☑ ⅛" (3mm), ⁷⁄₃₂" (5.5mm), ¼" (6mm) drill bits
- ☑ Countersink bit
- ☑ Hammer
- ☑ Awl to mark starter holes
- ☑ Screwdrivers to match screws

Engineering Advice:

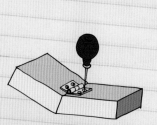
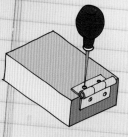

Place the hinge with the pin facing upward as shown. Push the bottom leaf of the hinge firmly against the end of the board. This will align the hinge pin with the edge of the board. Mark the holes on the top with the awl and insert screws. Push the two ends of the boards together. Mark the remaining holes and insert the screws.

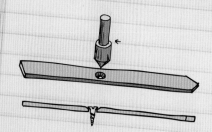

Use the countersink bit to countersink the holes for the skis so the screws don't scratch any surfaces.

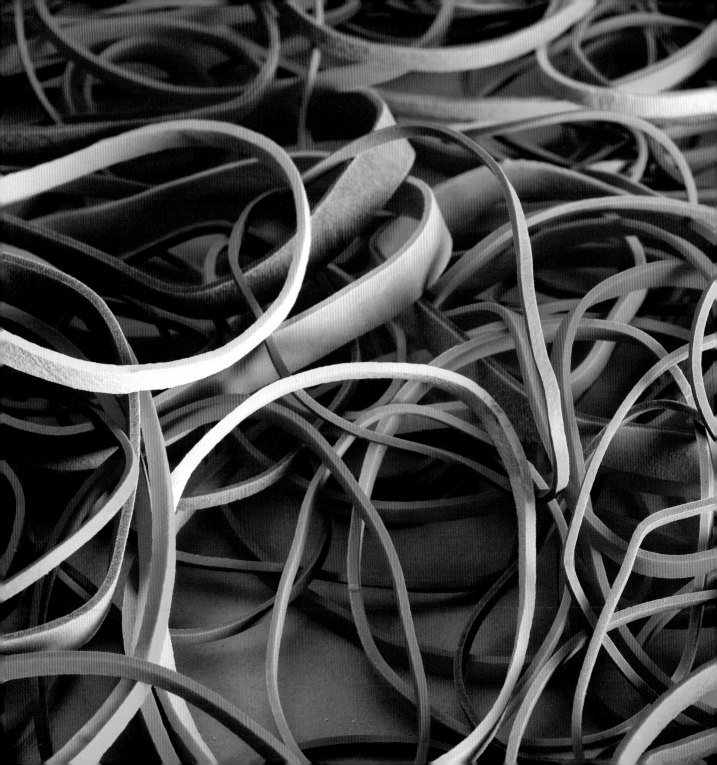

GAMES

The toys in this section come with all the trimmings
to make an entertaining game. Add a ball, make some
goalposts, follow the rules you know, or create your
own—and you have a fun way to spend an
afternoon. Try building the Golfinator (page 88),
10¢ Labyrinth Challenge (page 94), Mini-Croquet
(page 99), Hand Baseball (page 104), Hand Hockey
(page 109), and Hockey Man Target (page 115).

GOLFINATOR

Some people look at toys strewn all over the place and see a mess. Others, like us inventors, look at a pile of playhouses, blocks, dolls, toy kitchenware, and action figures and see a most amazing miniature golf course. You can make the Golfinator using basic tools in the same time it takes you to clean up after a good playtime. The Golfinator won't help clean up the mess, but he will transform it into a fantastic miniature golf course. Let everyone create one hole and you'll be playing "fore" hours!

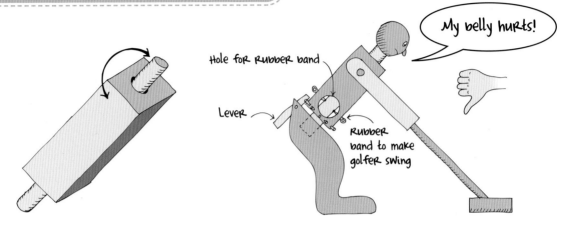

Rotating the torso:
The golfer's basic stance is feet shoulder-width apart, knees slightly bent, back leaning forward, arms straight, both hands on the golf club, and eyes on the ball. Then, the torso (stomach) rotates the upper body back to swing the club. This can be done with a dowel between the legs and the body.

Making a latch:
My first thought to create the swinging motion was to set the Golfinator's back swing and then push a button to make him swing. This could be done with a clever latch.

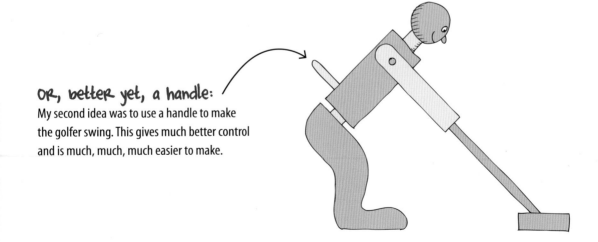

OR, better yet, a handle:
My second idea was to use a handle to make the golfer swing. This gives much better control and is much, much, much easier to make.

Golfinator

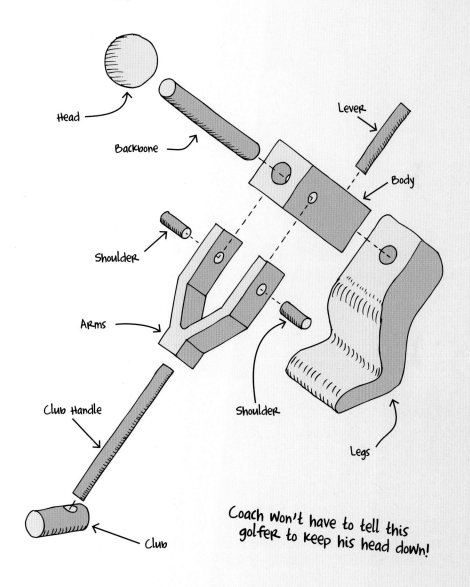

Head

Backbone

Lever

Body

Shoulder

Arms

Club Handle

Shoulder

Legs

Club

Coach won't have to tell this golfer to keep his head down!

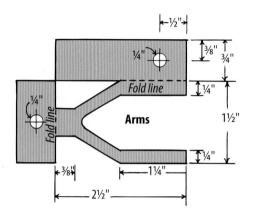

½"

⅜"

¾"

¼"

¼"

Fold line

Arms

¼"

Fold line

1½"

¼"

⅜"

1¼"

2½"

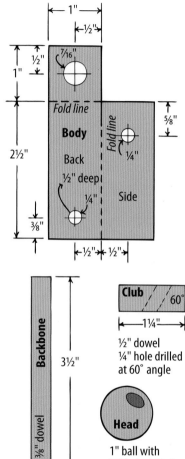

1"

½"

1"

½"

⁷⁄₁₆"

Fold line

Body

Back

½" deep

¼"

2½"

Side

⁵⁄₈"

¼"

⅜"

½" ½"

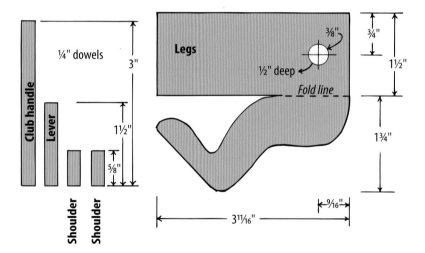

¼" dowels

Club handle

Lever

3"

1½"

⅝"

Shoulder

Shoulder

Legs

⅜"

½" deep

Fold line

¾"

1½"

1¾"

⁹⁄₁₆"

3¹¹⁄₁₆"

Backbone

3½"

⅜" dowel

Club   60°

1¼"

½" dowel
¼" hole drilled
at 60° angle

Head

1" ball with
⅜" hole drilled
½" deep

Inches
Millimeters

0 ¼ ½ ¾ 1 ¼ ½ ¾ 2

0 5 10 15 20 25 30 35 40 45 50

Enlarge pattern 175% for actual size.

Zany Wooden Toys that *Whiz, Spin, Pop,* and *Fly*

- ☑ 1½" (38mm) x 1¾" (44mm) x 3¹¹⁄₁₆" (94mm) pine board for legs (a.k.a. piece of 2 x 4)

- ☑ 1" (25mm) x 1" (25mm) x 2½" (64mm) board for body

- ☑ ¾" (19mm) x 1½" (38mm) x 2½" (64mm) for arms

- ☑ ½" (13mm) dowel, 1¼" (32mm) long for club

- ☑ ⅜" (10mm) dowel, 3½" (89mm) long for backbone

- ☑ ¼" (6mm) dowel, 7" (178mm) long for club handle, lever, and shoulders

- ☑ 1" (25mm) wooden ball to hold golfer's brain

- ☑ A small ball to golf with

- ☑ Coping saw

- ☑ Drill

- ☑ ¼" (6mm), ⅜" (10mm), and ⁷⁄₁₆" (11mm) drill bits

- ☑ Vise

Engineering Advice:

Try using a golf tee instead of a dowel for the lever. Tees are the perfect size, and they'll give your toy a touch of golfing class.

Be sure to give the shoulder pegs some extra space when hammering them in—that way, your golfer can move his arms to hit the ball at different heights.

Golf Course Ideas

Setting up your very own mini miniature golf course is a snap. Make curved paths using blocks or scrap wood, create ramps with books, and hit your balls into knocked-over mugs or holes cut in scrap wood. You are limited only by your imagination!

⅜" (10mm) dowel

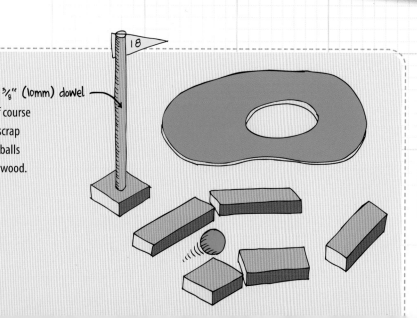

10¢ LABYRINTH CHALLENGE

Most people love a challenge—especially one they believe they can win. Let's make a pocket-size maze featuring a dime. Challenge people to get their dime through the hidden maze in one minute. If they succeed, you give them a dime. If they don't, then their dime is lost in the labyrinth for eternity (or until you can remove it).

Zany Wooden Toys that *Whiz, Spin, Pop,* and *Fly*

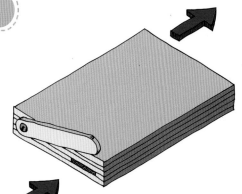

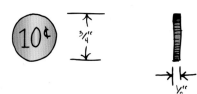

The dime: The dime is such a small coin for its value. This is good because it will allow us to make our labyrinth small and unassuming. The dime will fit easily through a slot ¾" (19mm) wide x ⅛" (3mm) tall. We'll cut the maze out of ⅛" (3mm) plywood.

The challenge: I don't want to pay out too many dimes, so the maze needs to be rather difficult in a very small area. Make it challenging by requiring the labyrinth to be flipped upside down. This means we'll need three layers for the maze, a layer for the top, and a layer for the bottom—a total of five layers of ⅛" (3mm) plywood.

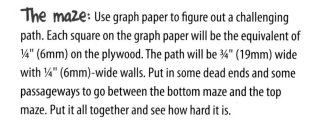

The maze: Use graph paper to figure out a challenging path. Each square on the graph paper will be the equivalent of ¼" (6mm) on the plywood. The path will be ¾" (19mm) wide with ¼" (6mm)-wide walls. Put in some dead ends and some passageways to go between the bottom maze and the top maze. Put it all together and see how hard it is.

10¢ Labyrinth Challenge

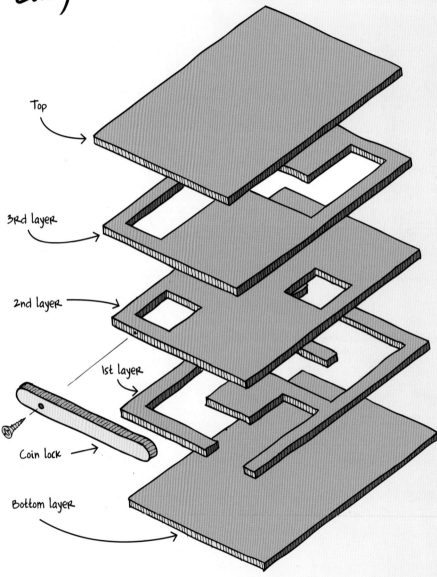

Top

3rd layer

2nd layer

1st layer

Coin lock

Bottom layer

1st layer

2nd layer

3rd layer

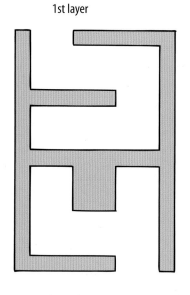

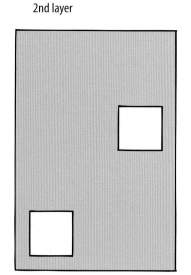

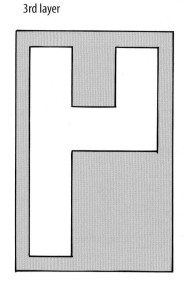

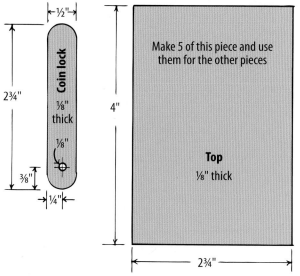

Coin lock

½"

2¾"

⅛" thick

⅛"

⅜"

¼"

4"

Make 5 of this piece and use them for the other pieces

Top
⅛" thick

2¾"

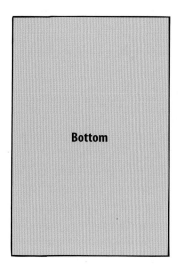

Bottom

Most dimensions ¼" or ¾"

Inches

Millimeters

0   ⅛ ¼ ⅜ ½ ⅝ ¾ ⅞ 1

0   5   10   15   20   25

Enlarge pattern 160% for actual size.

☑ ⅛" (3mm) x 2¾" (70mm) x 4" (102mm) pieces of plywood, 5

☑ ⅛" x ½" x 2¾" (3mm x 13mm x 70mm) piece of plywood for coin lock

☑ #4 x ½" (13mm) panhead screw

☑ White or yellow glue

☑ Dime

☑ Coping saw

☑ Drill

☑ ⅛" (3mm) drill bit

☑ Awl to mark starter holes

☑ Screwdriver to match screws

☑ Clamps to hold labyrinth (or heavy object to place on top of it) while the glue dries

Engineering Advice:

After you've cut out the pieces, make sure a dime will fit through all of the passageways.

Use as little glue as possible. If it squeezes into the maze, it might block the dime.

Con Artist's Advice:

Practice enough so you can do it behind your back with one hand. That'll convince anyone to try.

A small, rectangular box with a dime-size "goez-inta" and a "goez-outa"—it looks simple enough, so why not give it a try? Dime by dime, you'll patiently build your fortune. This is a fun toy to build, but a frustrating toy to play with. You can hear the dime moving and hitting walls, but add in the three-dimensional aspect, and it's downright maddening. A great way to make friends!

MINI-CROQUET

Croquet is a fun game, and it's just as much fun playing it on the floor with little croquet-people. Cut out a bunch of pieces and then start the fun with everyone decorating his or her own croquet-er (or whatever a professional croquet player is called). After you make the first player, you'll know the basic mechanics. From there, you can make the players taller or rounder, change the legs, or do whatever else is needed to add personality.

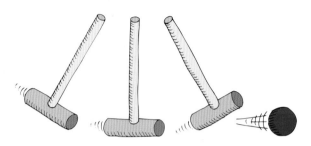

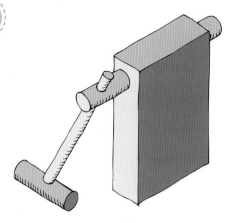

The mallet:
Croquet balls are hit straight on by swinging a mallet. Let's copy that exactly. Drill a ¼" (6mm) hole into a ½" (13mm) dowel to make a miniature mallet.

Swinging the mallet:
The mallet will have to be mounted on a pivot. Let's use a ½" (13mm) dowel as the pivot and put it into a block of wood.

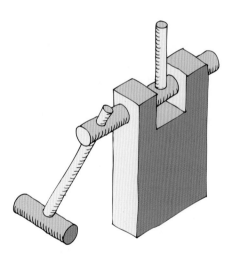

Controlling the mallet:
Croquet requires finesse, because sometimes you need to hit the ball a long way and other times, you need to gently tap the ball into position. This means that rubber bands, springs, and latches are out of the question. Let's just use a lever your finger can control.

The player:
We now have a mallet-swinging machine. Let's turn it into a fun-loving little person by adding some legs and a head. You can control the croquet-er with the head or the shoulders.

*Zany Wooden Toys that **Whiz, Spin, Pop**, and **Fly***

Mini-Croquet

Head

Neck

Shoulders

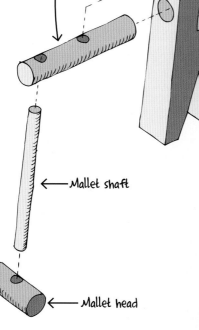

Body

Mallet shaft

Mallet head

Croquet is a great outdoor game in the summer. Now we've brought it inside in a shrunken version, so we can have a little family croquet match on the kitchen table or on the living room floor.

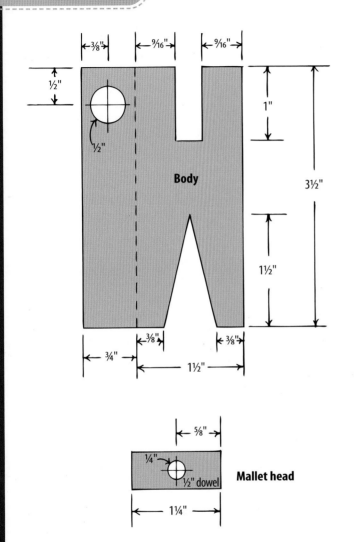

Body

3/8" 9/16" 9/16"

1/2"

1/2"

1"

3 1/2"

1 1/2"

3/8" 3/8"

3/4"

1 1/2"

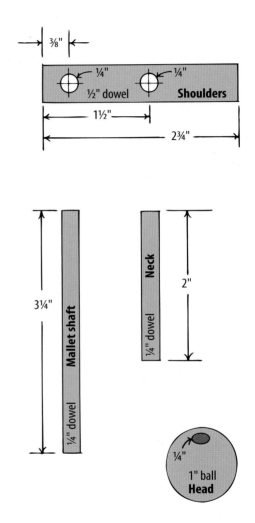

3/8"

1/4" 1/4"

1/2" dowel **Shoulders**

1 1/2"

2 3/4"

3 1/4"

1/4" dowel **Mallet shaft**

Neck

1/4" dowel

2"

1/4"

1" ball
Head

5/8"

1/4"

1/2" dowel **Mallet head**

1 1/4"

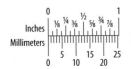

0   1/8 1/4 3/8 1/2 5/8 3/4 7/8   1

Inches

Millimeters

0   5   10   15   20   25

Enlarge pattern 130% for actual size.

Zany Wooden Toys that Whiz, Spin, Pop, and Fly

MATERIALS & TOOLS

- ☑ ³/₄" (19mm) x 1½" (38mm) x 3½" (89mm) pine board for body
- ☑ ½" (13mm) dowel, 4" (102mm) long for shoulders and mallet head
- ☑ ¼" (6mm) dowel, 5¼" (133mm) long for neck and mallet shaft
- ☑ 1" (25mm) diameter wooden ball for head and ball, 2
- ☑ Scrap wood for loops and post
- ☑ Scrap pieces of ¼" (6mm) dowel for post
- ☑ Coat hanger or other wire for loops (optional)
- ☑ Coping saw
- ☑ Drill
- ☑ ¼" (6mm) and ½" (13mm) drill bits

Croquet Course Ideas

Croquet is played by hitting your ball through hoops stuck in the grass and being the first to reach the post at the end of the course. The hoops can be made out of wood or with some coat hanger wire stuck into small blocks of wood. Try dowels in blocks of wood for the posts. Play a traditional game or build as many wickets as you want and make up your own rules! Maybe you can get the cat to stand still long enough...

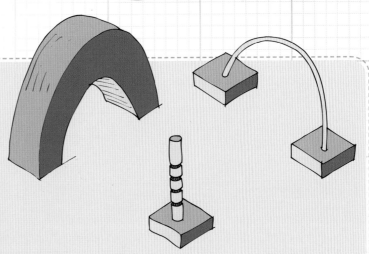

HAND BASEBALL

Anybody can have fun playing baseball. However, sometimes you can't get to a field or the weather doesn't cooperate. When that happens, it's time to move the game indoors. This toy will give you the same thrill, but on a much smaller scale. It can be built in the same time it takes to round up your friends, choose sides, and take the field. After you make the first batter, you won't even have to measure the ones that follow. Crank 'em out for all your friends.

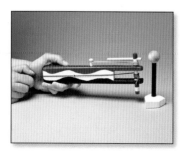

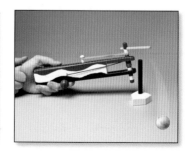

Zany Wooden Toys that *Whiz, Spin, Pop,* and *Fly*

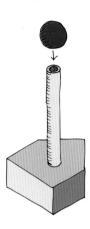

The pitch: Pitching would be pretty hard to do on a small scale. The ¾" (19mm) wooden ball would have to be moving pretty fast to stay in the air. Instead, let's put the ball on a batting tee to hit. Hitting it will still be mighty challenging.

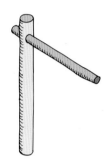

The bat: A ¼" (6mm) dowel should be able to smack a little ball a fair distance. Let's mount the bat in a ⅜" (10mm) dowel to swing it.

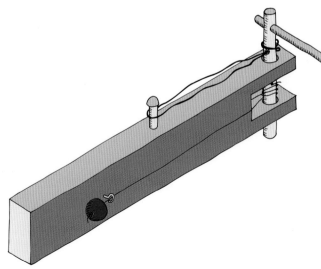

The batter: To swing the bat, we'll have to spin the ⅜" (10mm) dowel that holds the bat. Let's mount it in a piece of wood and attach a string. Pulling the string will spin the ⅜" (10mm) dowel and the bat. A rubber band will return the bat so we don't have to rewind the string after each swing.

HAND BASEBALL

Hand Baseball

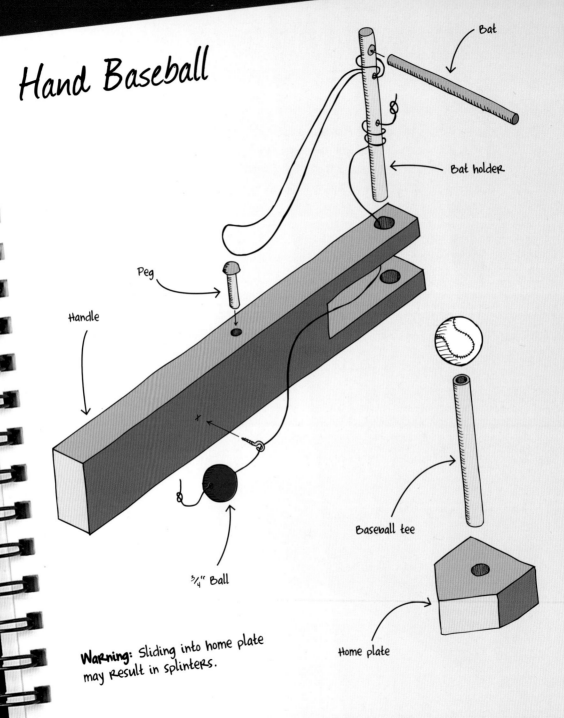

Bat

Bat holder

Peg

Handle

¾" Ball

Baseball tee

Home plate

Warning: Sliding into home plate may result in splinters.

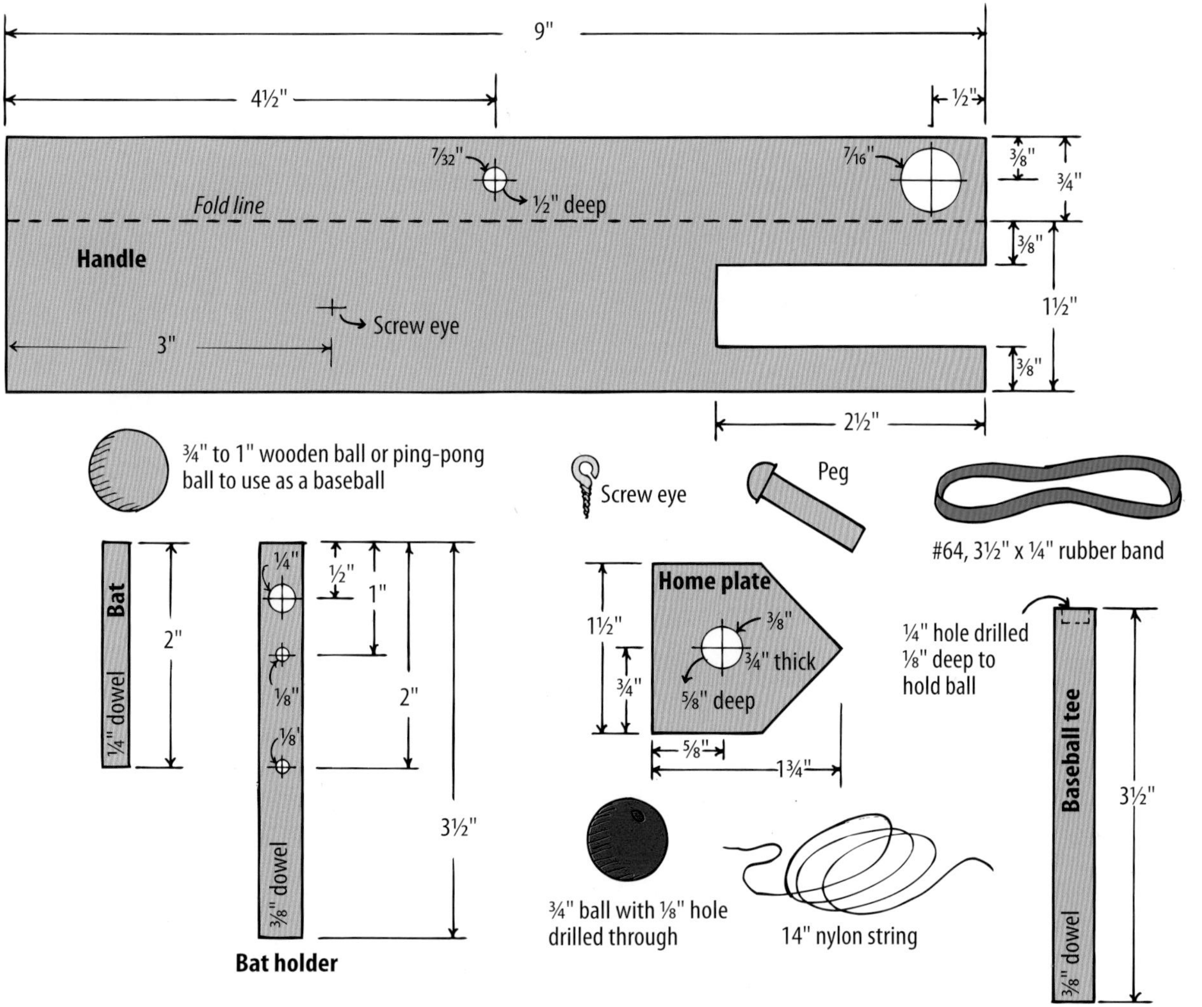
9"
4½"
½"
7⁄32"
½" deep
7⁄16"
⅜"
¾"
Fold line
Handle
⅜"
1½"
Screw eye
3"
⅜"
2½"
¾" to 1" wooden ball or ping-pong ball to use as a baseball
Screw eye
Peg
#64, 3½" x ¼" rubber band
Bat
¼" dowel
2"
¼"
½"
1"
⅛"
⅛"
2"
3½"
⅜" dowel
Bat holder
Home plate
1½"
⅜"
¾" thick
¾"
⅝" deep
⅝"
1¾"
¼" hole drilled ⅛" deep to hold ball
Baseball tee
3½"
⅜" dowel
¾" ball with ⅛" hole drilled through
14" nylon string

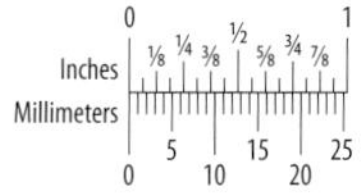
Inches
Millimeters

Enlarge pattern 170% for actual size.

☑ ³/₄" (19mm) x 1½" (38mm) x 11" (279mm) pine board for handle and home plate tee

☑ ³/₈" (10mm) dowel 7" (178mm) long for bat holder and tee

☑ ¼" (6mm) dowel, 3" (76mm) long for bat

☑ Peg

☑ ³/₄" (19mm) or 1" (25mm) wooden balls for string handle and baseball, 2

☑ 14" (356mm) nylon string

☑ ½" (13mm) screw eye

☑ #64, 3½" (89mm) x ¼" (6mm) rubber band

☑ Coping saw

☑ Drill

☑ ⅛" (3mm), ⁷/₃₂" (5.5mm), ¼" (6mm), ³/₈" (10mm), and ⁷/₁₆" (11mm) drill bits

☑ Awl to mark starter holes

☑ Needle-nose pliers (or strong fingers) to screw in eye screw

Ball Park Ideas

Let your mind go wild with this one. Get some empty cereal boxes and cut holes in them. The hole you hit the ball through determines the play. Make several big holes for singles, a few smaller holes for doubles, perhaps two holes for triples, and a hole for a pop fly out. Or use string to mark out areas on the carpet. Cut out little baseball players to field the ball, or cut a line in a wooden block to make a baseball card holder so your favorite pro players can field for you.

HAND HOCKEY

If you turn the Hand Baseball toy (page 104) upside down, it works great for hitting balls and pucks on the floor—like a hockey game. However, because hockey is such a fast game, you'll want to be able to dribble and shoot using only one hand.

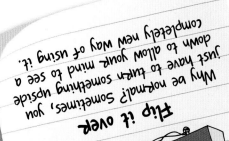

Flip it over

Why be normal? Sometimes, you just have to turn something upside down to allow your mind to see a completely new way of using it.

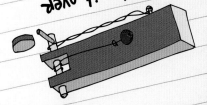

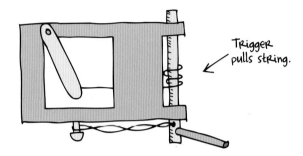

Trigger pulls string.

A taller base: Because we want to be able to operate the toy with one hand, we will need to make the base taller.

The trigger: The best way to get the hockey stick to move is to make a trigger to pull a string and swing the blade.

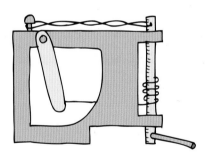

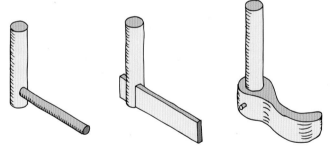

A wider base: Make the base wider so that the base, not the hockey stick, rests on the ground. This will make it easier to dribble and shoot.

The blade: The dowel bat is easy to make, but does not work very well for dribbling because it does not rest on the floor. Let's try other materials. A slat does not work well because the groove is hard to make and loose-fitting. A curved blade, cut from a board, with a ⅜" (10mm) hole fits very well on the dowel and can easily be substituted.

HAND HOCKEY

Hand Hockey

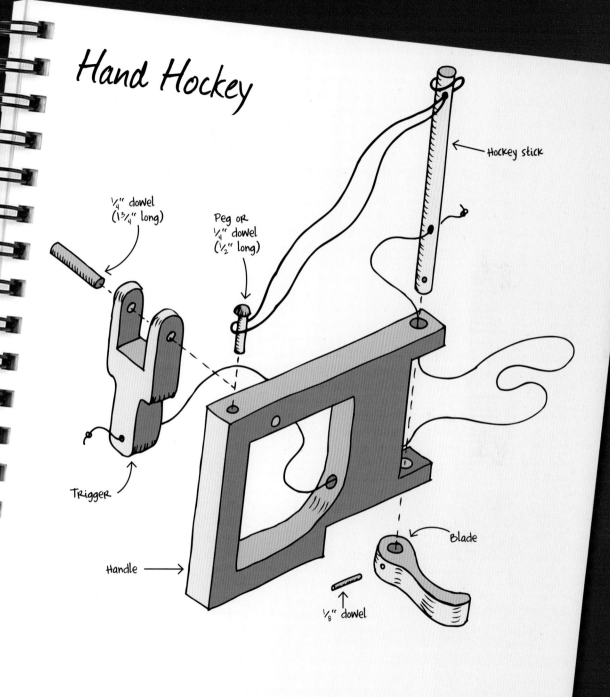

¼" dowel
(1¾" long)

Peg or
¼" dowel
(½" long)

Hockey stick

Trigger

Handle

Blade

⅛" dowel

PATTERNS

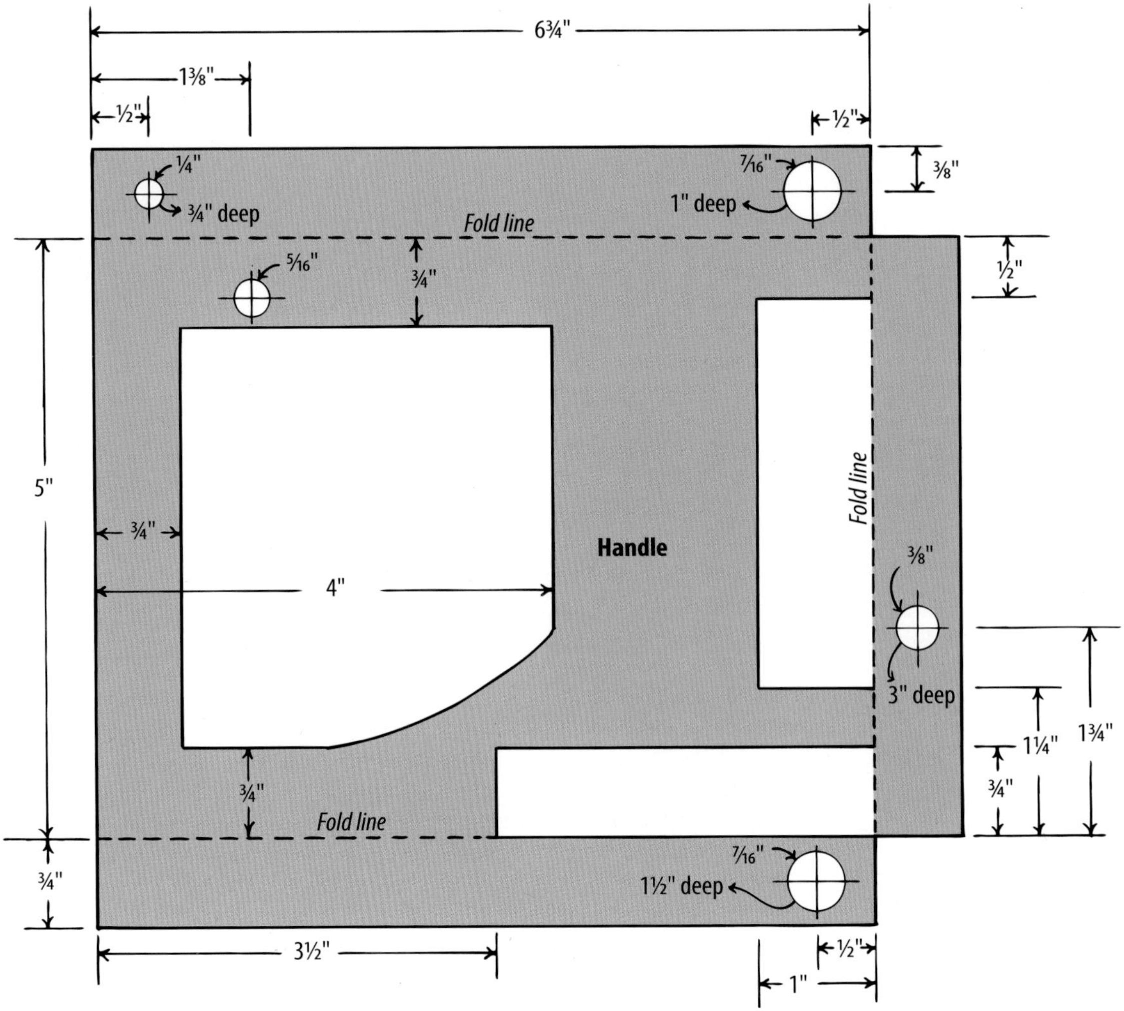

6¾"
1⅜"
½"
½"
¼"
¾" deep
7⁄16"
1" deep
⅜"
Fold line
5⁄16"
¾"
½"
5"
Fold line
Handle
¾"
4"
⅜"
3" deep
1¼"
1¾"
¾"
¾"
Fold line
¾"
7⁄16"
1½" deep
3½"
½"
1"

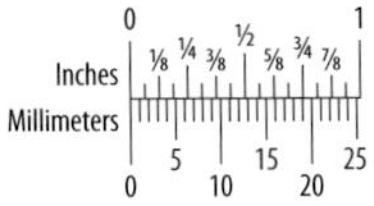

Inches
Millimeters
0
⅛
¼
⅜
½
⅝
¾
⅞
1
5
10
15
20
25

Enlarge pattern 160% for actual size.

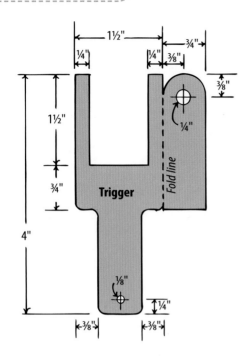

Trigger

Fold line

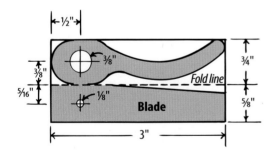

Blade

Fold line

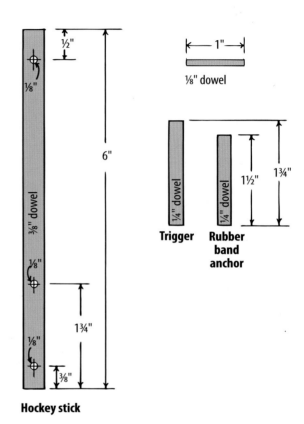

Hockey stick

⅛" dowel

Trigger   **Rubber band anchor**

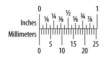

Inches
Millimeters

Enlarge pattern 160% for actual size.

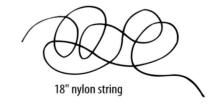

18" nylon string

☑ $3/4$" (19mm) x 5" (127mm) x $6\frac{3}{4}$" (171mm) pine board for handle

☑ $3/4$" (19mm) x $1\frac{1}{2}$" (38mm) x 4" (102mm) pine board for trigger

☑ $3/4$" (19mm) x $3/4$" (19mm) x 3" (76mm) pine board for blade

☑ $3/8$" (10mm) dowel, 6" (152mm) long for hockey stick

☑ $1/4$" (6mm) dowel, 4" (102mm) long for trigger and rubber band anchor

☑ $1/8$" (3mm) dowel 1" (25mm) long or $3/4$" (19mm) nail to attach hockey blade

☑ 18" (457mm) nylon string

☑ 1" (25mm) wheels or $1/4$" (6mm)-thick pieces of 1" (25mm) dowel for pucks

☑ Coping saw

☑ Drill

☑ $1/8$" (3mm), $1/4$" (6mm), $5/16$" (8mm), $3/8$" (10mm), and $7/16$" (11mm) drill bits

☑ Hammer

☑ Thin wire for pulling rubber band and strings

Engineering Advice:

Make pucks out of 1" (25mm) store-bought wheels or cut off $1/4$" (6mm)-thick pieces of 1" (25mm) dowel. Sand them so they glide. Create a goal for each player by cutting a U from a board.

Want a high-speed game of hockey on the kitchen floor? This toy will put some serious speed on a little wooden puck. There is one internal cut that may take a little time, but it's worth the effort.

HAND HOCKEY

Zany Wooden Toys that Whiz, Spin, Pop, and Fly

Hockey Man
TARGET

Fun and a little twisted is the only way to describe this toy. It is easy to make, fun to paint, and hysterically funny to play. The face changes with each successful shot. Make this for your sport fanatic as a reminder to wear his or her mouth guard. This target goes along nicely with the Hand Hockey Toy (page 109). Or you can make your own little hockey stick to use with it.

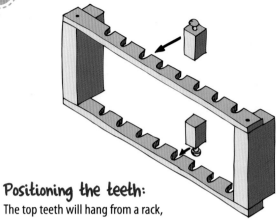

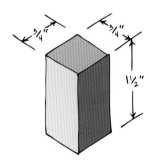

The teeth: All teeth should be identical so you don't have to sort them out. Start with teeth that are ¾" (19mm) x ¾" (19mm) x 1½" (38mm).

Positioning the teeth:
The top teeth will hang from a rack, and the bottom teeth will sit on a shelf. Put a peg in each tooth. Slots will position the teeth. There should be about ¼" (6mm) between the top and bottom rows of teeth.

The face: Make a face out of ½" (13mm) plywood and cut open a mouth large enough to expose all the teeth.

The base: Add a plywood base to hold the face up, and build a ramp out of thin cardboard to launch the pucks into the mouth.

← Hand hockey, page 109

Hockey Man Target

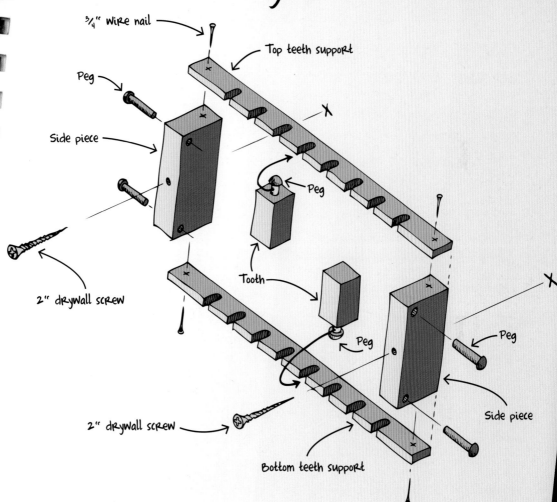

3/4" wire nail

Top teeth support

Peg

Side piece

Peg

Tooth

2" drywall screw

Peg

2" drywall screw

Peg

Side piece

Bottom teeth support

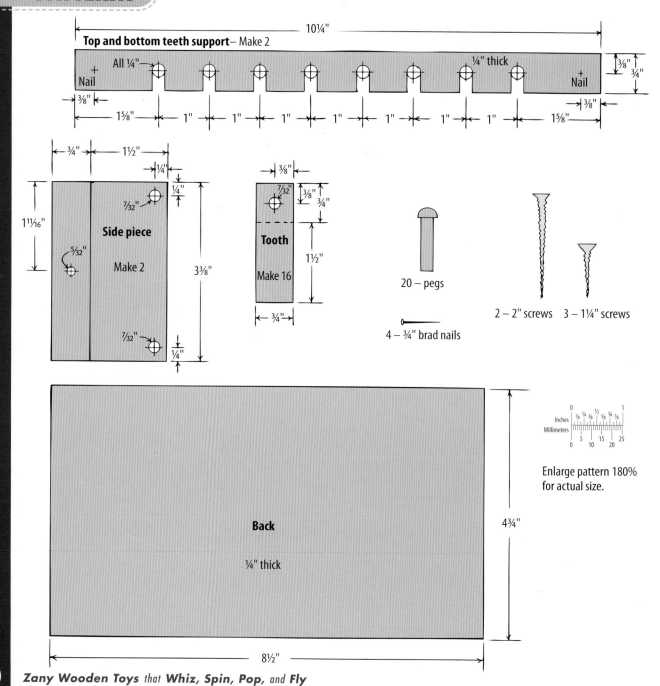

Top and bottom teeth support– Make 2

10¼"

All ¼"

¼" thick

Nail

Nail

⅜" / ¾"

⅜"

⅜"

1⅝" — 1" — 1" — 1" — 1" — 1" — 1" — 1" — 1⅝"

¾" — 1½"

¼"

¼"

7/32"

1¹¹/₁₆"

Side piece

Make 2

5/32"

3⅜"

7/32"

¼"

⅜"

7/32"

⅜" / ¾"

Tooth

Make 16

1½"

¾"

20 – pegs

2 – 2" screws   3 – 1¼" screws

4 – ¾" brad nails

Back

¼" thick

4¾"

8½"

0   ¼   ½   ¾   1
Inches   ⅛ ¼ ⅜ ½ ⅝ ¾ ⅞
Millimeters
0   5   10   15   20   25

Enlarge pattern 180% for actual size.

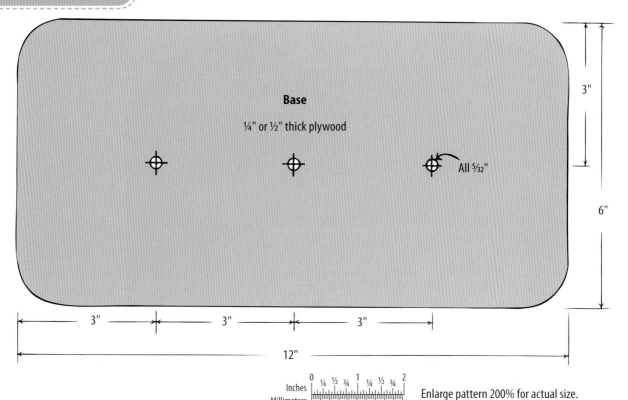

Base

¼" or ½" thick plywood

All ⁵⁄₃₂"

3"

6"

3"   3"   3"

12"

Inches
Millimeters

Enlarge pattern 200% for actual size.

HeRe's another good game to play. It's called "Team Dentist." The objective is to put all the teeth back in the shortest time possible—from the front. Knock yourself out!

HOCKEY MAN TARGET

119

Arrange the face any way you want it. Drill ¼" holes for the eyebrows to allow them to be raised or lowered to change his mood from happy to annoyed. Glue all other pieces in place.

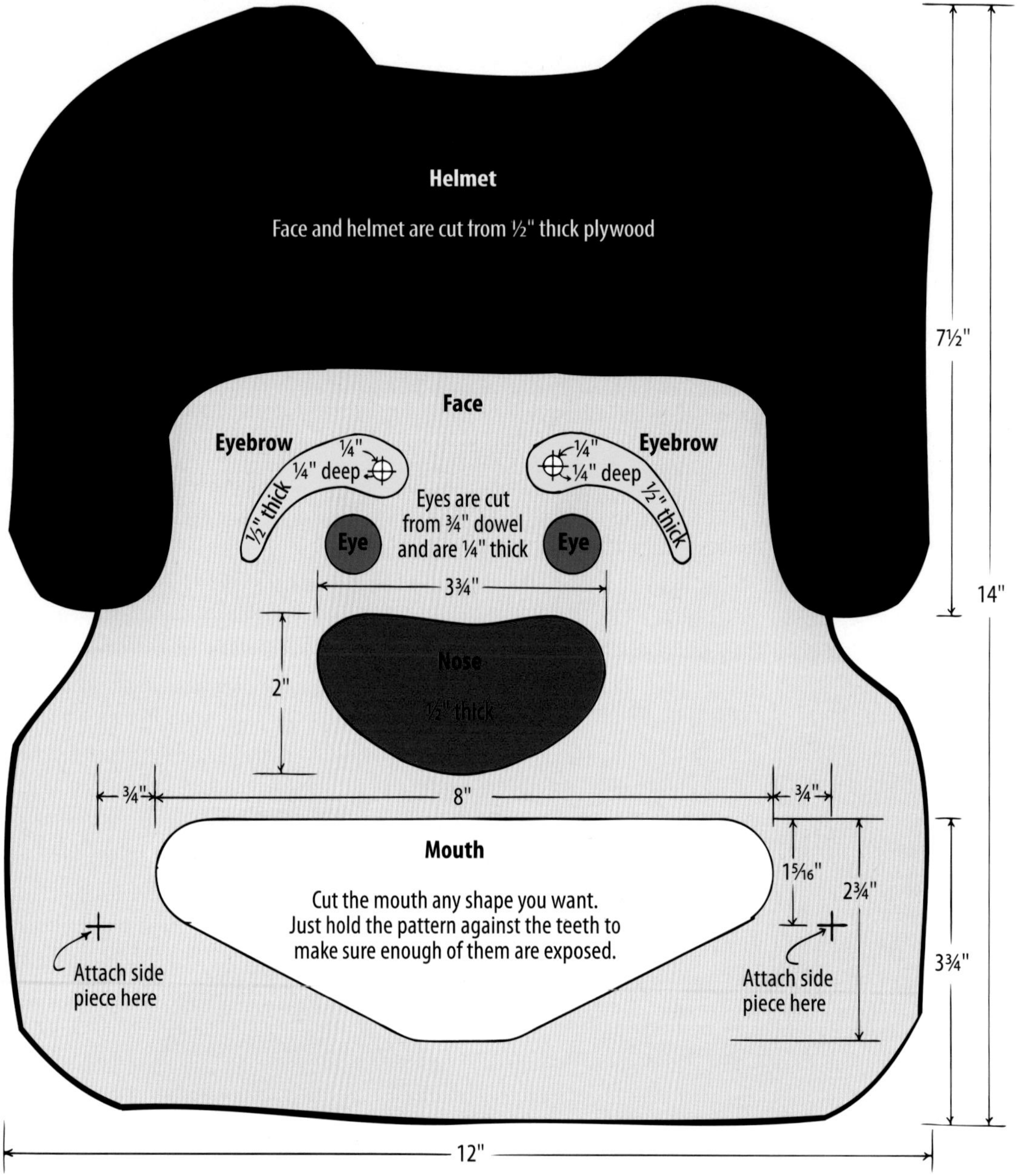

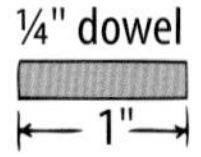

Helmet

Face and helmet are cut from ½" thick plywood

7½"

14"

Face

Eyebrow ¼" ¼" deep ½" thick

Eyebrow ¼" ¼" deep ½" thick

Eyes are cut from ¾" dowel and are ¼" thick

Eye

Eye

3¾"

Nose

½" thick

2"

¾"

8"

¾"

Mouth

Cut the mouth any shape you want. Just hold the pattern against the teeth to make sure enough of them are exposed.

Attach side piece here

Attach side piece here

1⁵⁄₁₆"

2¾"

3¾"

12"

¼" dowel

← 1" →

Make 2 for eyebrow pivots

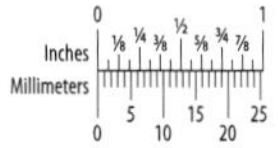

Inches
Millimeters

Enlarge pattern 225% for actual size.

- ☑ ³⁄₄" (19mm) x 1½" (38mm) x 7" (178mm) pine board for side pieces

- ☑ ³⁄₄" (19mm) x ³⁄₄" (19mm) x 25" (635mm) pine board for teeth

- ☑ ½" (13mm) x 12" (305mm) x 20" (508mm) plywood for face and base

- ☑ ¼" (6mm) x 4¾" (121mm) x 8½" (216mm) plywood for back

- ☑ ¼" (6mm) x ¾" (19mm) x 21" (533mm) plywood for top and bottom teeth supports

- ☑ ¼" (6mm) dowel, 2" (51mm) long for eyebrow pivots

- ☑ Scrap wood for eyebrows, eyes, and nose

- ☑ Pegs, 20

- ☑ ³⁄₄" (19mm) wire nails with heads, 4

- ☑ 2" (51mm) drywall screws, 2

- ☑ 1¼" (32mm) drywall screws, 3

- ☑ 8½" (216mm) x 11" (279mm) thin cardboard for ramp (from back of notebook)

- ☑ 1" (25mm) diameter store-bought wheels for pucks

- ☑ Coping saw

- ☑ Crosscut saw

- ☑ Drill

- ☑ ⁵⁄₃₂" (4mm), ⁷⁄₃₂" (5.5mm), and ¼" (6mm) drill bits

- ☑ Hammer

- ☑ Screwdriver to match screws

Engineering Advice:

Ideally, this toy should be portable. To keep the teeth from falling out when transporting the target, drill holes in the side pieces, and insert pegs to hold a ¼" (6mm) piece of plywood against the back of the teeth. The ramp can also be stored back there.

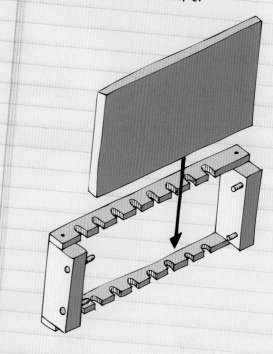

TOYS

Here's the place to look if you want a toy that requires some imagination to play with it. Whether you're looking for a single vehicle to carry you over land, sea, and air (The Ultimate Adventurer's Vehicle, page 126), a tool to help you dig to the other side of the world (Mine Shaft Digger, page 134), an airplane you can pilot yourself (Airplane on a Stick, page 139), a wild motorcycle that does all the coolest tricks you can think of (Extreme Motorcycle, page 144), your very own camera that can capture the real and the imaginary (U-Draw Instamatic Camera, page 149), or a robot to carry out your bidding (Ball-and-Socket Robot, page 156), you've come to the right pages. Let's build some toys—make sure you bring your tools and your imagination!

While I was driving somewhere, my noggin sprouted an idea.

What if my car could take me anywhere and get me out of any danger?

It would need to drive on roads, float on water, and fly.

And when all your luck has run out, it's gotta have one more trick up its sleeve...

The Ultimate
ADVENTURER'S VEHICLE

Yeah, this toy looks a little fussy, but remember, it's really four toys in one. It's worth the effort. Although there are quite a few pieces, they are all very straightforward to make. Also, you don't have to make them all in one trip to the shop. Make the truck first. Later you can cut out the wings or add the boat. How cool would it be to keep modifying the same toy? The boat and the hovercraft can be held on with tape or rubber bands. Save the detailed work for the scheduled 100,000-mile maintenance.

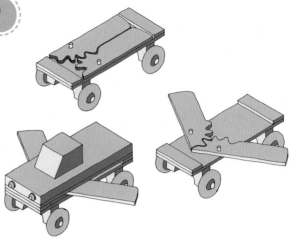

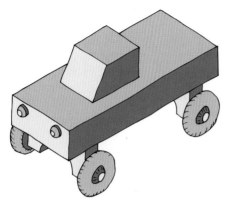

The truck: When all of the special features are hidden, this toy looks like an innocent but sturdy four-wheel-drive truck capable of hauling a month's worth of supplies and scientific instruments deep into the heart of the jungle.

The plane: The vehicle will need wings that fold out to fly over a cliff or an impassable canyon. Use a gear mechanism so both wings unfold at the same time.

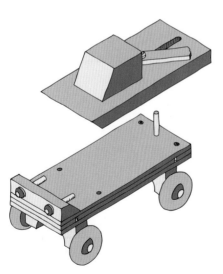

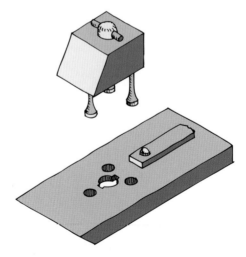

The boat: Make the top of the truck a detachable boat. Secure the boat to the truck using a latch. The pegs of the headlights insert into the front of the boat to hold it in place.

The hovercraft: Turn the cab into an emergency hovercraft, using golf tees as the thrusters and a keyed latch to keep the hovercraft connected until needed.

The Ultimate Adventurer's Vehicle

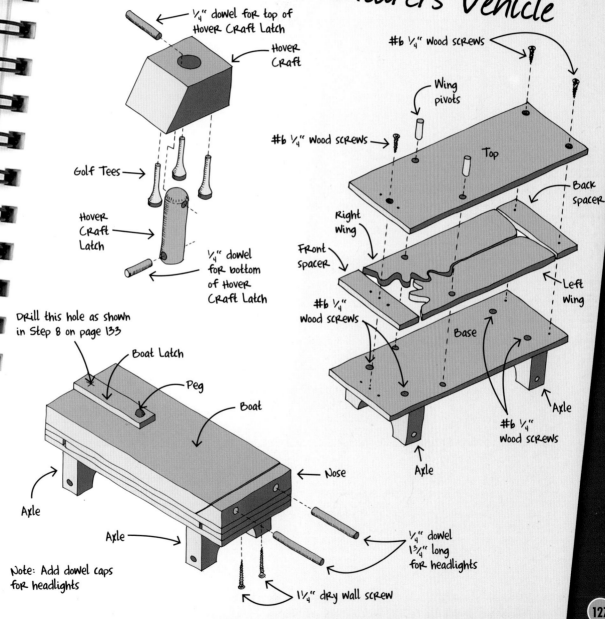

¼" dowel for top of Hover Craft Latch

Hover Craft

#b ¼" Wood screws

Wing pivots

#b ¼" Wood screws

Top

Golf Tees

Back spacer

Hover Craft Latch

Right Wing

¼" dowel for bottom of Hover Craft Latch

Front spacer

Left Wing

#b ¼" Wood screws

Drill this hole as shown in Step 8 on page 133

Base

Boat Latch

Peg

Boat

Axle

Nose

#b ¼" Wood screws

Axle

Axle

Axle

¼" dowel 1¾" long for headlights

Note: Add dowel caps for headlights

1¼" dry wall screw

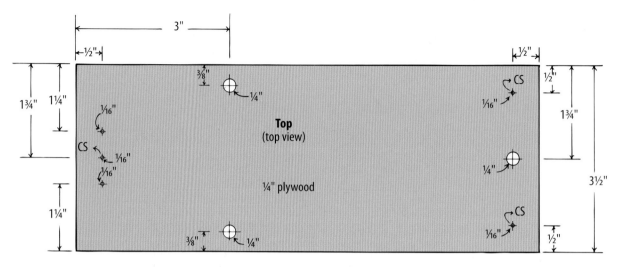

3"

½"

1¾" 1¼"

⅜"

¼"

1/16"

CS

1/16"

1/16"

Top
(top view)

¼" plywood

½"

1¾"

CS

1/16"

¼"

1¼"

⅜"

¼"

CS

1/16"

½"

3½"

½"

"CS"=countersink   "CSOS"=countersink opposite side

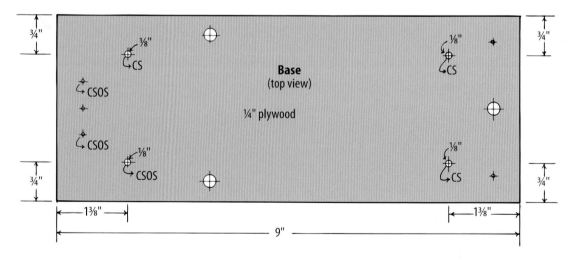

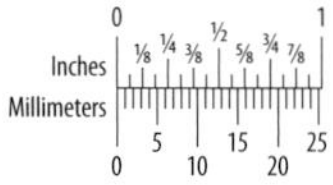

¾"

⅛"

CS

CSOS

CSOS

⅛"

CSOS

Base
(top view)

¼" plywood

¾"

⅛"

CS

⅛"

CS

¾"

¾"

1⅜"

1⅜"

9"

Inches
Millimeters

0 ⅛ ¼ ⅜ ½ ⅝ ¾ ⅞ 1
0   5   10   15   20   25

Enlarge pattern 180% for actual size.

Zany Wooden Toys that *Whiz, Spin, Pop,* and *Fly*

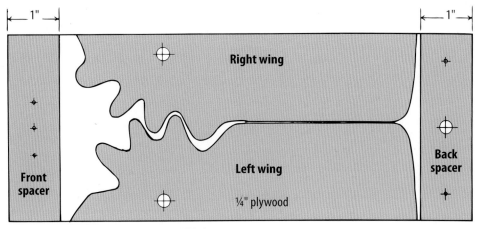

All holes same as top

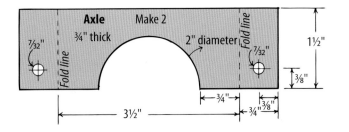

Inches ⅛ ¼ ⅜ ½ ⅝ ¾ ⅞

Millimeters 5 10 15 20 25

Enlarge pattern 180% for actual size.

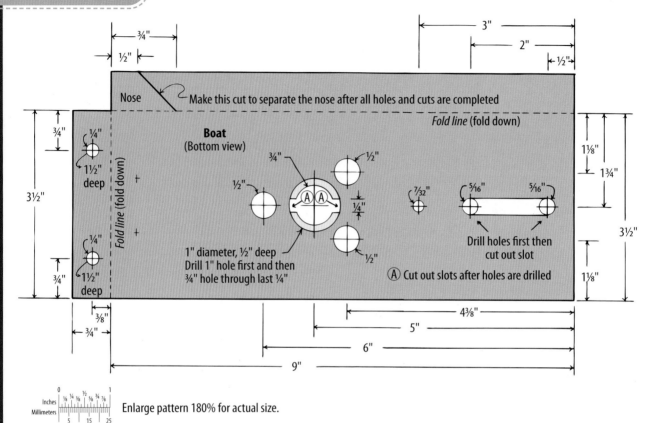

Nose — Make this cut to separate the nose after all holes and cuts are completed

Boat
(Bottom view)

Fold line (fold down)

1" diameter, ½" deep
Drill 1" hole first and then
¾" hole through last ¼"

Ⓐ Cut out slots after holes are drilled

Drill holes first then
cut out slot

Fold line (fold down)

Enlarge pattern 180% for actual size.

With the addition of your imagination,
this groovy vehicle can escape from a
herd of rampaging elephants, fly to
Antarctica, float down rivers of molten
cheese on planet Cheddaratica, and
hover over your best friend's head.
Where is your toy going to go?

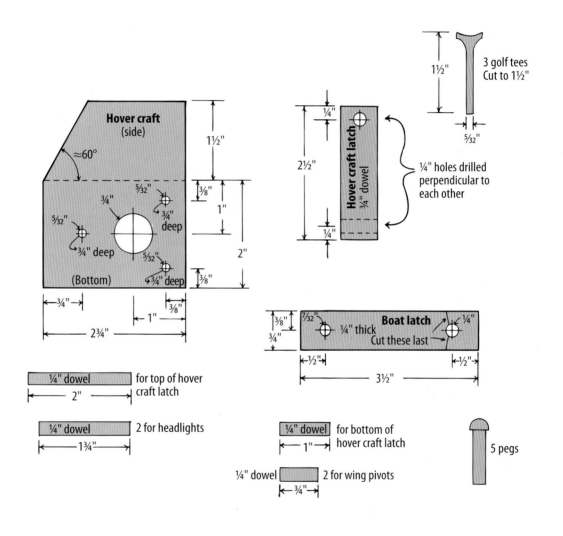

Hover craft
(side)

≈60°

5/32"

3/4"

3/4" deep

5/32"

3/4" deep

5/32"

3/4" deep

(Bottom)

1½"

3/8"

1"

2"

3/8"

3/4"

1"

3/8"

2¾"

1/4"

2½"

1/4"

Hover craft latch
3/4" dowel

1½"

3 golf tees
Cut to 1½"

5/32"

¼" holes drilled
perpendicular to
each other

3/8"

7/32"

3/4"

1/4" thick

Boat latch

1/4"

Cut these last

½"

3½"

½"

¼" dowel — for top of hover
craft latch

2"

¼" dowel — 2 for headlights

1¾"

¼" dowel — for bottom of
hover craft latch

1"

¼" dowel — 2 for wing pivots

3/4"

5 pegs

0   1
Inches   1/8   1/4   3/8   1/2   5/8   3/4   7/8
Millimeters
0   5   10   15   20   25

Enlarge pattern 180% for actual size.

- ☑ ¼" (6mm) x 3½" (89mm) x 9" (229mm) plywood for truck body and wings, 3

- ☑ ¾" (19mm) x 3½" (89mm) x 9" (229mm) pine board for boat

- ☑ ¾" (19mm) x 1½" (38mm) x 7" (178mm) pine board for axles

- ☑ ¼" (6mm) x ¾" (19mm) x 3½" (89mm) pine board for boat latch

- ☑ 1½" (38mm) x 2" (51mm) x 2¾" (70mm) piece of 2 x 4 pine board for hovercraft

- ☑ 2" (51mm)-diameter wheels, ½" (13mm) to ¾" (19mm) thick, 4

- ☑ ¾" (19mm) diameter dowel, 2½" (64mm) long for hovercraft latch

- ☑ ¼" (6mm) dowel, 8" (203mm) long

- ☑ Pegs, 5

- ☑ Golf tees, 3

- ☑ Dowel caps for headlights, 2

- ☑ #6 x ¾" (19mm) wood screws, 7

- ☑ 1¼" (32mm) drywall screws, 2

- ☑ Coping saw

- ☑ Miter saw

- ☑ Miter box

- ☑ Drill

- ☑ ¹⁄₁₆" (2mm), ⅛" (3mm), ⁵⁄₃₂" (4mm), ⁷⁄₃₂" (5.5mm), ¼" (6mm), ⁵⁄₁₆" (8mm), ½" (13mm), ¾" (19mm), 1" (25mm), and countersink drill bits

- ☑ Hammer

- ☑ Screwdrivers to match screws

- ☑ Clamp or vise

- ☑ Sandpaper

- ☑ Tape

GETTING IT TOGETHER

1 Cut out three pieces of ¼" (6mm)-thick x 3½" (89mm) x 9" (229mm) plywood for the base, wings, and top. Mark the seven holes with a pencil or awl, as shown, on the top piece of ¼" (6mm) plywood, and then tape the pieces together. Drill through all three pieces at the same time.

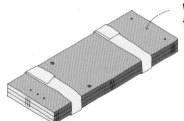

Do not drill this hole yet

2 Use a pencil to make three hash marks on the front and three sets of hash marks on the side. This will help realign the parts after they are separated.

3 Remove the tape, and cut out the wings. Sand the wings so they slide smoothly between the base and top pieces.

4 Drill the ⅛" (3mm) holes in the base. Countersink the holes as shown in the patterns.

Zany Wooden Toys that Whiz, Spin, Pop, and Fly

5 Connect the base to the axles using four of the #6 x ¾" (19mm) wood screws.

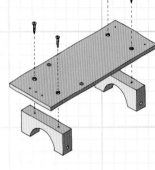

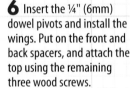

6 Insert the ¼" (6mm) dowel pivots and install the wings. Put on the front and back spacers, and attach the top using the remaining three wood screws.

7 Cut out the ¾" (19mm)-thick pine board for the boat and drill the holes for the headlights. Drill the ⁷⁄₃₂" (5.5mm) hole for the peg. Now, make the diagonal cut for the front of the boat.

8 Attach the nose to the front of the truck using the two 1¼" (32mm) drywall screws. Attach the boat latch to the boat using a peg. Attach the boat to the truck by inserting the two ¼" (6mm) dowels for the headlights. Align the latch, and drill the ¼" (6mm) hole through the latch, the boat, and the three layers of plywood.

Drill after assembly

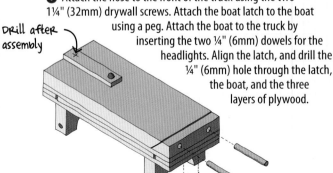

9 Remove the latch, and cut off the end according to the plans. The hole is the perfect distance from the peg. Next, widen the ¼" (6mm) hole in the boat to ⁵⁄₁₆" (8mm), and cut out the slot. The boat latch is now complete.

10 Remove the boat and the latch. Flip the boat upside down, and drill a 1" (25mm)-diameter hole ½" (13mm) deep as shown. Next, drill a ¾" (19mm)-diameter hole on the same center. Use the coping saw to add the notches for the keyed latch.

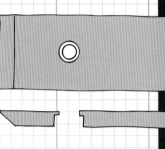

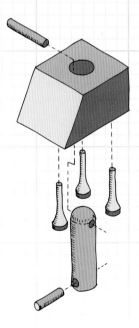

11 Make the hovercraft according to the plans. Drill three ⁵⁄₃₂" (4mm) holes in the boat for the hovercraft's thrusters. Put the 2½" (64mm)-long ¾" (19mm)-diameter dowel in the hovercraft, and insert a 1" (25mm)-long piece of ¼" (6mm)-diameter dowel in the bottom hole and a 2" (51mm)-long piece in the top hole. The bottom dowel should fit into the notches of the boat. Twisting the top dowel 90° will latch the hovercraft to the boat.

Mine Shaft
DIGGER

Sand can provide you with countless hours of fun making castles, roads, and mountains. Eventually, there's the need to dig a deep hole or a tunnel through a mountain of sand. Sure, your hand will work, but you are limited by the length of your arm—and that may not be long enough. So let's make the ultimate sandbox hole-digging tool.

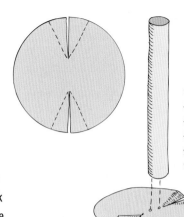

The drill bit: We'll use a Mason jar lid, orange juice can lid, or almost any other round metal lid. Make two cuts toward the center of the round disk on opposite sides. Bend one side of the cut down and the other side up. Be sure to bend back the edges so they are not sharp. Attach the disk to the end of a dowel using two screws. When you twist the disk into the sand, one side will be digging into the sand while the other is pushing the sand out of the hole.

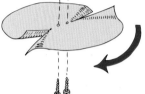

Note: Be sure to bend back the edges of the metal lid so there are no sharp edges.

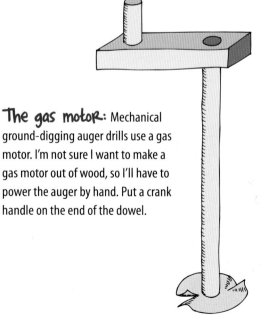

The gas motor: Mechanical ground-digging auger drills use a gas motor. I'm not sure I want to make a gas motor out of wood, so I'll have to power the auger by hand. Put a crank handle on the end of the dowel.

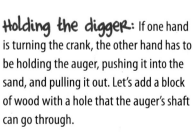
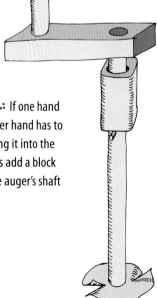

Holding the digger: If one hand is turning the crank, the other hand has to be holding the auger, pushing it into the sand, and pulling it out. Let's add a block of wood with a hole that the auger's shaft can go through.

Mine Shaft Digger

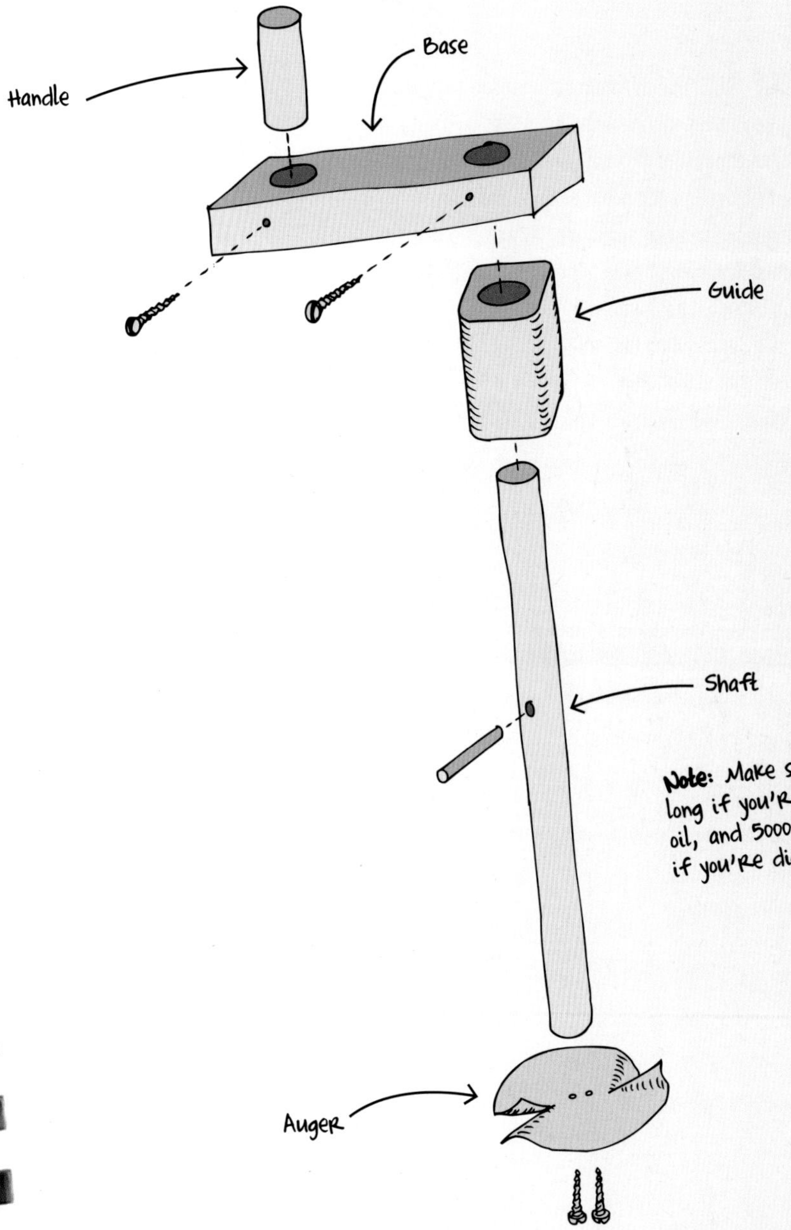

Handle

Base

Guide

Shaft

Note: Make shaft 500 feet (150 meters) long if you're planning on drilling for oil, and 5000 feet (1500 meters) long if you're digging to China.

Auger

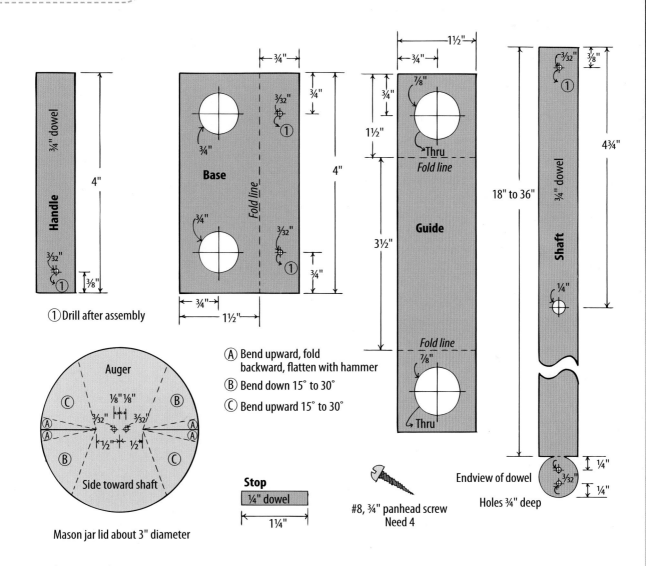

Handle

¾" dowel

4"

³⁄₃₂"
① ⅜"

① Drill after assembly

Base

¾"

³⁄₃₂"
①

¾"

¾"

4"

³⁄₃₂"
①

¾"

¾"

1½"

Fold line

Auger

⅛" ⅛"

³⁄₃₂"   ³⁄₃₂"

Ⓒ   Ⓑ

Ⓐ   Ⓐ
Ⓐ   Ⓐ

½" ½"

Ⓑ   Ⓒ

Side toward shaft

Mason jar lid about 3" diameter

Ⓐ Bend upward, fold
backward, flatten with hammer

Ⓑ Bend down 15° to 30°

Ⓒ Bend upward 15° to 30°

Stop

¼" dowel

1¼"

#8, ¾" panhead screw
Need 4

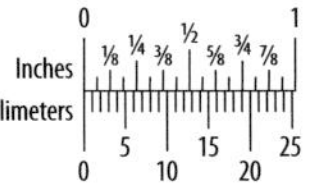

1½"

¾"

⅞"
Thru

¾"

1½"

3½"

Guide

Fold line

Fold line

⅞"
Thru

¾"

³⁄₃₂"
①

⅜"

18" to 36"

4¾"

¼"

¾" dowel

Shaft

¼"

Endview of dowel

Holes ¾" deep

Ⓒ
³⁄₃₂"
Ⓒ

¼"

0   Inches   1
⅛ ¼ ⅜ ½ ⅝ ¾ ⅞
Millimeters
0 5 10 15 20 25

Enlarge pattern 175% for actual size.

- ☑ 1½" (38mm) x 1½" (38mm) x 3½" (89mm) pine board for guide
- ☑ ¾" (19mm) x 1½" (38mm) x 4" (102mm) pine board for base
- ☑ ¾" (19mm) dowel, 18" (457mm) to 36" (914mm) long for shaft and handle
- ☑ 3" (76mm)-diameter piece of sheet metal—preferably a Mason jar lid or juice can lid, because the edges are smooth
- ☑ #8 x ¾" (19mm) panhead screws, 4
- ☑ Saw
- ☑ Drill
- ☑ ³⁄₃₂" (2.5mm), ¼" (6mm), ¾" (19mm), and ⅞" (22mm) drill bits
- ☑ Tin snips for cutting lid
- ☑ Needle-nose pliers for bending lid

Engineering Advice:

Bend about ¼" (6mm) of the cut edge on the metal lid over on itself, and flatten it to get rid of the sharp edge.

The auger easily digs into the sand, but it is not strong enough to lift a lot. So just dig a few inches at a time and then clear the sand out of the hole.

I saw a guy digging postholes for a fence using a tool that looked like a huge drill bit connected to a gas-powered motor. It quickly bored nice, clean holes several feet deep in the earth. I thought, "Wouldn't that be fun to have at the beach or in a sandbox when you want to make a tunnel or dig a mine shaft?"

AIRPLANE ON A STICK

Yea, this toy looks too simple to be any fun—but looks can be deceiving. The joystick allows you to bank, roll, climb, dive, and do all types of aerial maneuvers (without getting dizzy). Just build it and see for yourself!

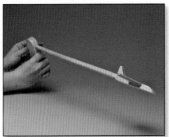

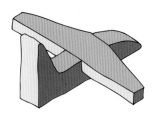

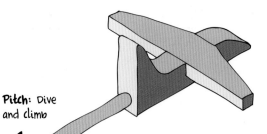

Pitch: Dive and climb

Roll: Left and Right bank turns

The basic plane: Let's build a very basic airplane for now—just a body and wings. We can make a fancy one later if we want.

Roll and pitch: The easiest way to roll a plane is to put a dowel straight out the back. Turning the dowel will roll the plane left and right. The dowel also will control the pitch for climbing and diving.

The joystick: Add the joystick to the back of the dowel so it will control the airplane.

The handle: Let's add a handle to hold the control dowel so it's easier to fly.

PATTERNS

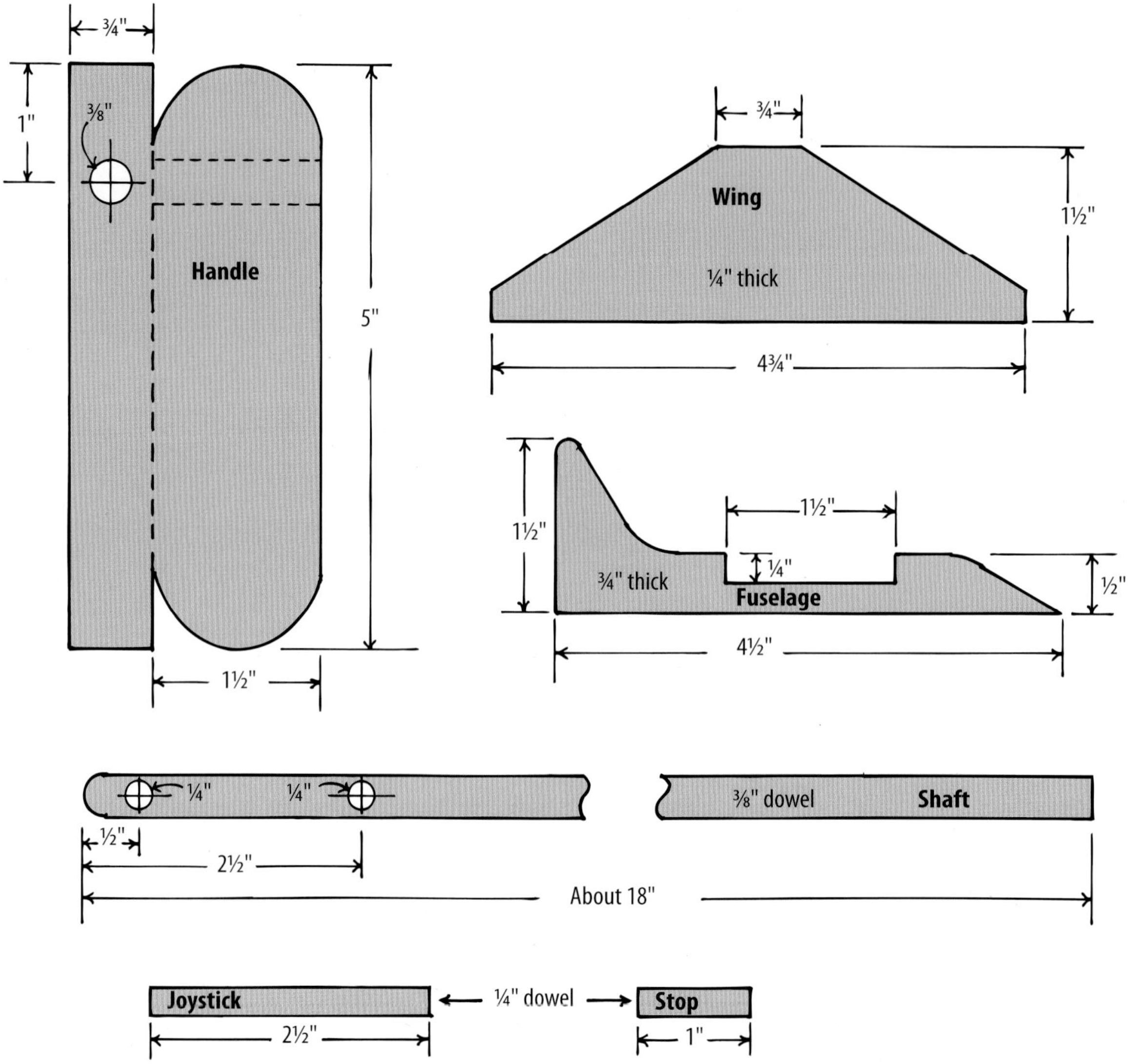
¾"
1"
⅜"
Handle
5"
1½"
¾"
Wing
¼" thick
1½"
4¾"
1½"
1½"
¼"
¾" thick
Fuselage
½"
4½"
¼"
¼"
⅜" dowel
Shaft
½"
2½"
About 18"
Joystick
¼" dowel
Stop
2½"
1"

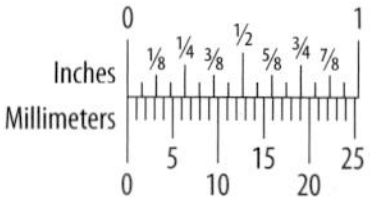
Inches
Millimeters

Enlarge pattern 160% for actual size.

- ☑ ¾" (19mm) x 1½" (38mm) x 10" (254mm) pine board for fuselage and handle

- ☑ ¼" (6mm) x 1½" (38mm) x 4¾" (121mm) pine board for wings

- ☑ ⅜" (10mm) dowel, 18" (457mm) long for shaft

- ☑ ¼" (6mm) dowel, 3½" (89mm) long for joystick and stop

- ☑ Glue if needed for attaching wings

- ☑ Coping saw

- ☑ Drill

- ☑ ¼" (6mm) and ⅜" (10mm) drill bits

Engineering Advice:

Drill the hole into the back of the plane before you cut out the shape. This makes it easier to drill the hole straight.

Glue the wings to the fuselage if they are too loose.

Don't glue the control dowel into the back of the airplane. This way, you can swap out different planes.

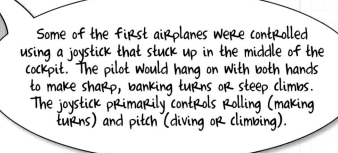

Some of the first airplanes were controlled using a joystick that stuck up in the middle of the cockpit. The pilot would hang on with both hands to make sharp, banking turns or steep climbs. The joystick primarily controls rolling (making turns) and pitch (diving or climbing).

Extreme
MOTORCYCLE

Before you start to make this motorcycle, go outside, find a little dirt patch, mix up a little mud, and make a racetrack complete with jumps, bumps, and banked turns. Then, go get your tools, and start this project. You'll be finishing up just as the track dries out. I recommend using wide craft sticks (tongue depressors) for the front and rear forks, but paint sticks, 1/8" (3mm) plywood, or any thin wood will work. Drill the holes for the nails in the forks to prevent the wood from splitting. Everyone's first thought is the forks will be too weak and will break, but they are actually quite strong. However, at some point, you'll do something too extreme and end up having to take your cycle back to the shop for repair. The good news is you won't have to spend any time in the hospital.

TOY INVENTOR'S WORKSHOP

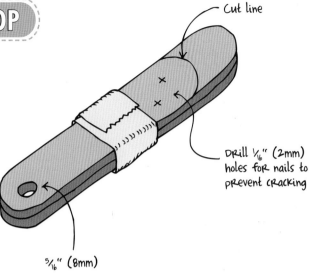

Cut line

× ×

× ×

Drill ¹⁄₁₆" (2mm) holes for nails to prevent cracking

⁵⁄₁₆" (8mm)

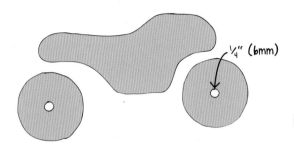

¼" (6mm)

The motorcycle: Let's make the body out of a ¾" (19mm)-wide board and use 2" (51mm)-diameter wooden wheels. These wheels will have a ¼" (6mm) hole so that a ¼" (6mm) dowel will fit snugly into them. To make the wheels turn freely, the holes in the forks will have to be slightly larger, about ⁵⁄₁₆" (8mm).

The front and rear forks: Attaching the wheels is the hard part. We need something strong but thin; otherwise, our motorcycle will look too bulky. Let's try craft sticks. These are thin and are made from a hard wood. We'll have to cut them down to size, though. To make sure they are perfectly matched, tape two of them together, and do all of the cutting and drilling at the same time.

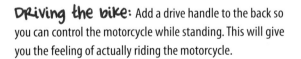

Driving the bike: Add a drive handle to the back so you can control the motorcycle while standing. This will give you the feeling of actually riding the motorcycle.

The handlebar: This is just a basic T-shape. Use a ½" (13mm) dowel for the steering column and a ¼" (6mm) dowel for the handlebar.

Zany Wooden Toys that Whiz, Spin, Pop, and Fly

EXTREME MOTORCYCLE

145

Extreme Motorcycle

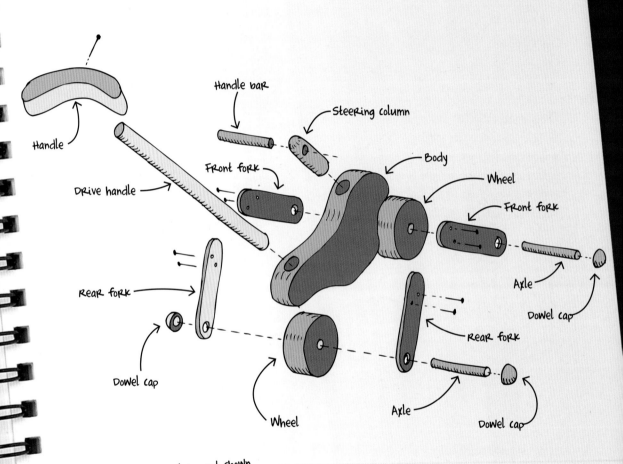

Handle

Handle bar

Steering column

Drive handle

Front fork

Body

Wheel

Front fork

Rear fork

Axle

Dowel cap

Dowel cap

Rear fork

Wheel

Axle

Dowel cap

Note: Front left dowel cap not shown

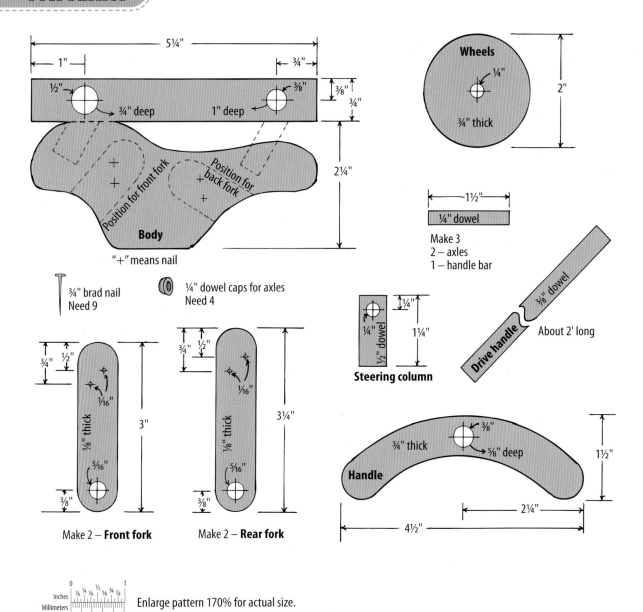

Wheels
1/4"
2"
3/4" thick

5 1/4"
1"
3/4"
1/2"
3/8"
3/4" deep
1" deep
3/8"
3/4"
2 1/4"

Position for front fork
Position for back fork

Body

"+" means nail

3/4" brad nail
Need 9

1/4" dowel caps for axles
Need 4

1 1/2"
1/4" dowel

Make 3
2 – axles
1 – handle bar

1/4"
1/4" dowel
1 1/4"
1/2" dowel

Steering column

3/8" dowel

Drive handle
About 2' long

3/4" 1/2"
1/16"
1/8" thick
3"
5/16"
3/8"

Make 2 – **Front fork**

3/4" 1/2"
1/16"
1/8" thick
3 1/4"
5/16"
3/8"

Make 2 – **Rear fork**

3/8"
3/4" thick
5/8" deep
1 1/2"

Handle

2 1/4"
4 1/2"

0   1/4 1/2 3/4 1
1/8 3/8 5/8 7/8
Inches
Millimeters
0   5   10   15   20   25

Enlarge pattern 170% for actual size.

EXTREME MOTORCYCLE

- ☑ ³/₄" (19mm) x 2¼" (57mm) x 5¼" (133mm) pine board for body
- ☑ ³/₄" (19mm) x 1½" (38mm) x 4½" (114mm) pine board for handle
- ☑ 2" (51mm) wheels, ³/₄" (19mm)-thick, with ¼" (6mm) holes, 2
- ☑ Wide craftsticks for forks, 4 (plus a few extras in case they break)
- ☑ ½" (13mm) dowel, 2" (51mm) long for steering column
- ☑ ³/₈" (10mm) dowel, 24" (610mm) long for drive handle
- ☑ ¼" (6mm) dowel, 5" (127mm) long for handlebars and axles
- ☑ Dowel caps for the axles, 4
- ☑ ³/₄" (19mm) wire nails with heads, 9
- ☑ Coping saw
- ☑ Drill
- ☑ ¹/₁₆" (2mm), ¼" (6mm), ⁵/₁₆" (8mm), ³/₈" (10mm), and ½" (13mm) drill bits
- ☑ Hammer
- ☑ Tape

Engineering Advice:

Drill the ½" (13mm) hole for the handlebar steering column and the ³/₈" (10mm) hole for the drive handle into the body of the motorcycle before you cut out the shape. Since these holes are drilled at an angle, it is easier to drill when you have a flat edge as a reference to create the angle.

Don't glue the drive handle into the motorcycle. Instead, make it fit snugly, using a piece of tape on the end of the dowel. This way the bike can be played with by hand.

> The stunts people do on motorcycles these days are amazing! They go flying off huge ramps and race around gnarly dirt tracks. Experiment with some cool tricks and races on your extreme motorcycle!

EXTREME MOTORCYCLE

U-Draw Instamatic
CAMERA

This is a fun project to make, but the real fun begins when you start "taking" pictures. You've made a self-contained art studio for your next vacation trip.

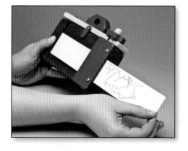

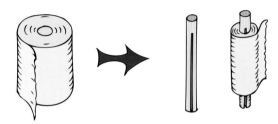

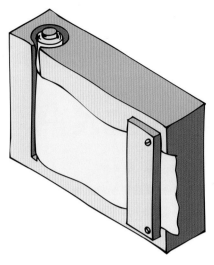

The film: Even though we will be hand drawing our pictures, we still want to advance the film for the next picture. Thus, we need a very long, skinny piece of paper. A roll of cash register paper fits the bill.

The camera: The paper must unroll across a flat drawing surface. Make the body of the camera from a 2 x 4. Drill a hole to hold the roll of paper, and attach a piece of wood to clamp the paper in place.

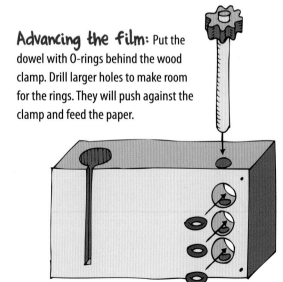

Advancing the film: Put the dowel with O-rings behind the wood clamp. Drill larger holes to make room for the rings. They will push against the clamp and feed the paper.

Taking pictures: There's a lot of solid wood in the camera. Let's drill some holes to hold pencils and crayons for drawing pictures. Finish off the camera with a viewfinder, lid, and lens.

U-Draw Instamatic Camera

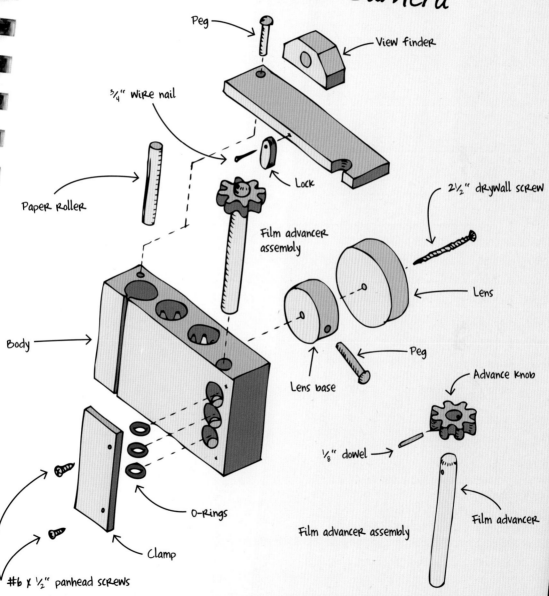

Peg

View finder

¾" wire nail

Paper Roller

Lock

Film advancer assembly

2½" drywall screw

Lens

Body

Peg

Lens base

Advance Knob

⅛" dowel

Film advancer

O-Rings

Film advancer assembly

Clamp

#6 x ½" panhead screws

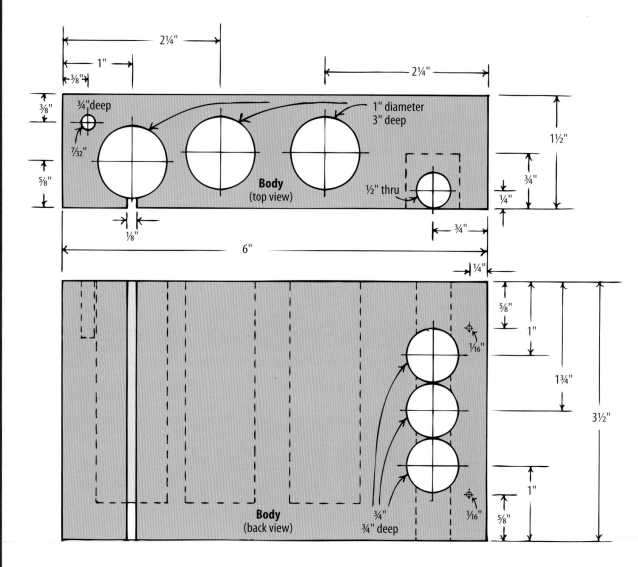

Body
(top view)

¾"deep

¾" diameter
3" deep

½" thru

Body
(back view)

¾"
¾" deep

Inches
Millimeters

Enlarge pattern 130% for actual size.

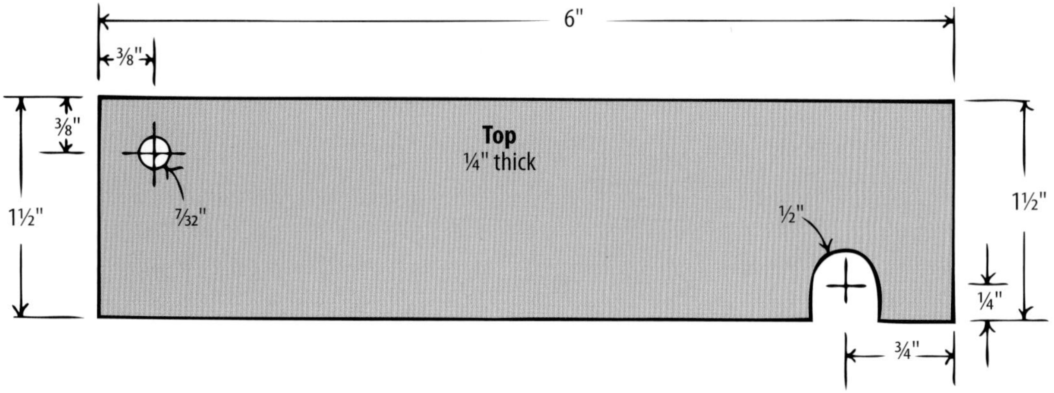
6"
3/8"
3/8"
Top
1/4" thick
7/32"
1 1/2"
1/2"
1 1/2"
1/4"
3/4"

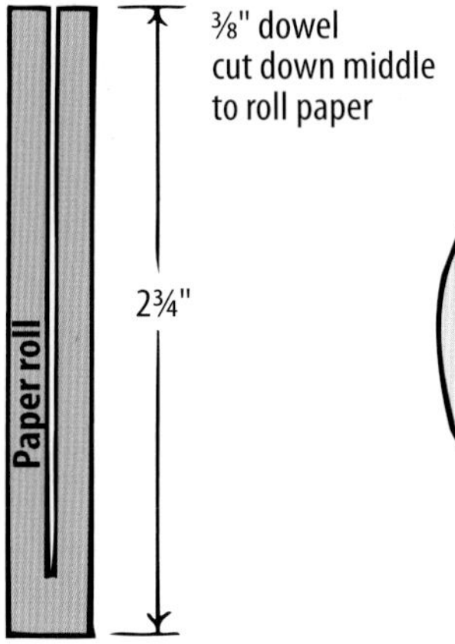
3/8" dowel
cut down middle
to roll paper
2 3/4"
Paper roll

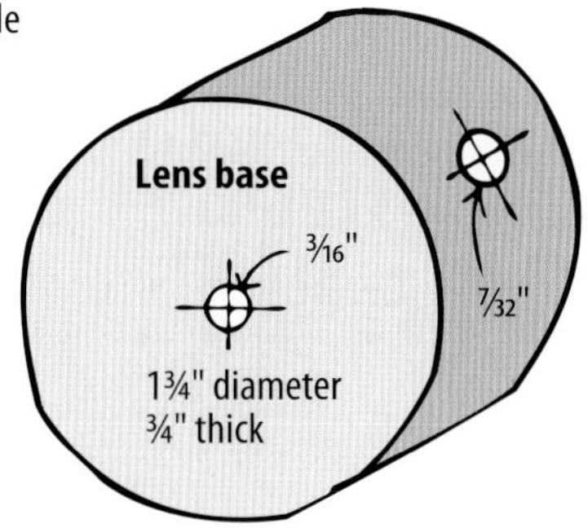
Lens base
3/16"
7/32"
1 3/4" diameter
3/4" thick

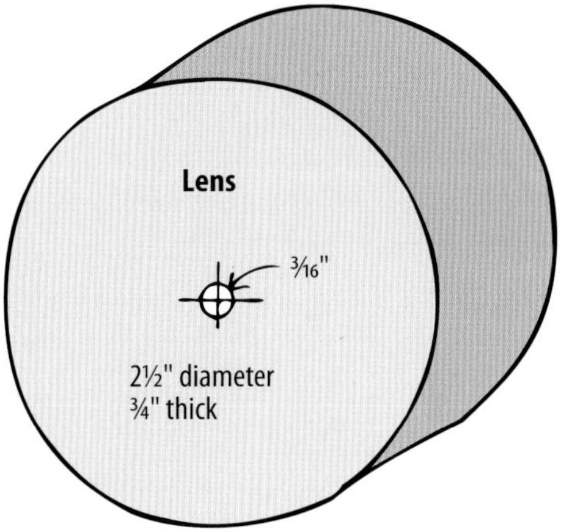
Lens
3/16"
2 1/2" diameter
3/4" thick

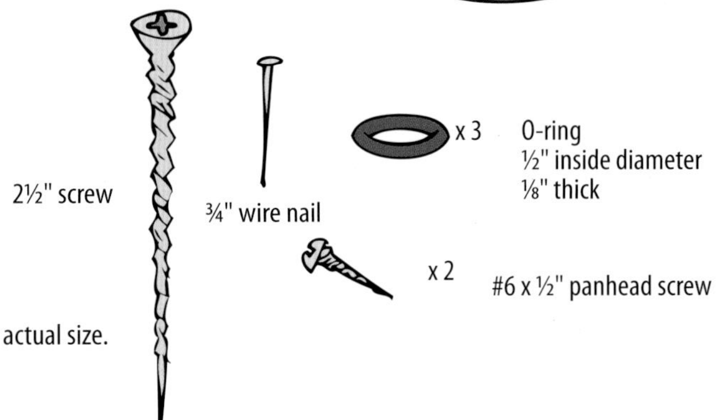
2 1/2" screw
3/4" wire nail
x 3
O-ring
1/2" inside diameter
1/8" thick
x 2
#6 x 1/2" panhead screw

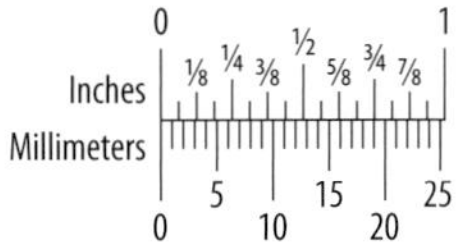
0
1
1/8
1/4
3/8
1/2
5/8
3/4
7/8
Inches
Millimeters
0
5
10
15
20
25

Enlarge pattern 130% for actual size.

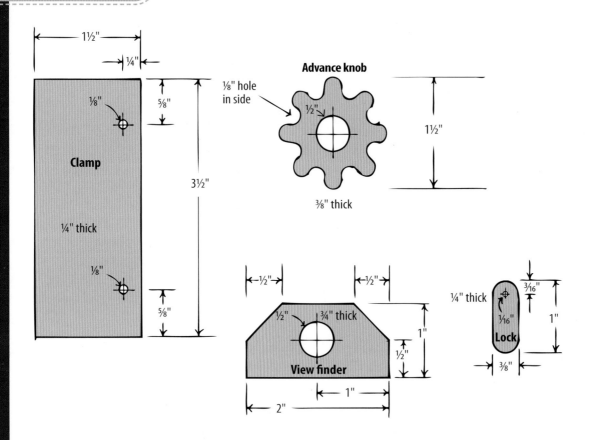

Clamp

1½"

¼"

⅛"

5/8"

3½"

¼" thick

⅛"

5/8"

Advance knob

⅛" hole in side

½"

1½"

3/8" thick

View finder

½"

½"

¾" thick

1"

½"

2"

1"

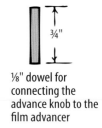

¼" thick

3/16"

1/16"

Lock

1"

3/8"

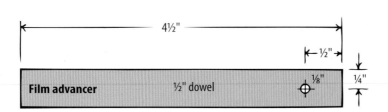

Film advancer   ½" dowel

4½"

½"

⅛"

¼"

¾"

⅛" dowel for connecting the advance knob to the film advancer

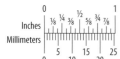

Inches

Millimeters

0   ⅛ ¼ 3/8 ½ 5/8 ¾ 7/8   1

0   10   20

5   15   25

Enlarge pattern 130% for actual size.

*Zany Wooden Toys that **Whiz, Spin, Pop,** and **Fly***

U-DRAW INSTAMATIC CAMERA

MATERIALS & TOOLS

- ☑ 1½" (38mm) x 3½" (89mm) x 6" (152mm) piece of 2 x 4 pine board for the camera body
- ☑ ¾" (19mm) x 2½" (64mm) x 10" (254mm) pine board for lens, lens base, viewfinder, and advance knob
- ☑ ¼" (6mm) x 1½" (38mm) x 10½" (267mm) pine board for top, clamp, and lock
- ☑ ½" (13mm) dowel, 4½" (114mm) long for film advancer
- ☑ ⅛" (3mm) dowel, ¾" (19mm) long
- ☑ ⅜" (10mm) dowel, 2¾" (70mm) long for paper roll
- ☑ Pegs, 2
- ☑ ½" (13mm) inside diameter, ⅛" (3mm)-thick O-Rings, 3
- ☑ 2½" (64mm) drywall screw
- ☑ #6 x ½" (13mm) panhead screw
- ☑ ¾" (19mm) wire nail
- ☑ Cash register tape, 2" (51mm) wide
- ☑ Pencils
- ☑ Crayons
- ☑ Coping saw
- ☑ Miter saw
- ☑ Miter box
- ☑ Drill
- ☑ 1/16" (2mm), ⅛" (3mm), 3/16" (5mm), 7/32" (5.5mm), ½" (13mm), ¾" (19mm), and 1" (25mm) drill bits
- ☑ Hammer
- ☑ Screwdriver to match screws

Engineering Advice:

To decide what type of wheel I wanted to grip and advance the paper, I experimented with different materials. You can try other options, too: Just hold the dowel with your fingers, apply a downward force, and rotate. Does the material pull the paper?

First try: Rubber bands doubled-over many times. This was not very consistent in pulling the paper, but it worked.

Second try: Duct tape rolled onto a dowel. The smooth surface didn't pull very well. However, roughening the surface with coarse sandpaper did make it work.

Third try: O-Rings from the plumbing store. They gripped the paper very well. Let's use these.

Ball-and-Socket
ROBOT

The ball-and-socket joint is the basic building block for this toy. Each joint requires only a few holes and some straight cuts. However, you'll need to make quite a few, so set them up like an assembly line for mass production. There's an easy way to do this, as you'll see. Then, have fun personalizing your robot with various attachments. After you're done, move on to a Robo-dog or Robo-spider.

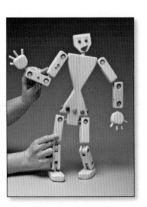

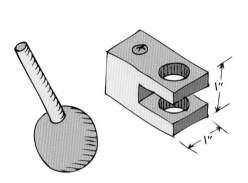

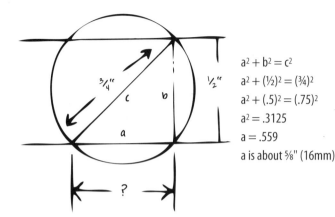

$$a^2 + b^2 = c^2$$
$$a^2 + (½)^2 = (¾)^2$$
$$a^2 + (.5)^2 = (.75)^2$$
$$a^2 = .3125$$
$$a = .559$$

a is about ⅝" (16mm)

The basic joint: To make the ball of the joint, we'll use a ¾" (19mm)-diameter ball with a ¼" (6mm) hole on a ¼" (6mm) dowel. The socket will be 1" (25mm) x 1" (25mm) with a hole drilled to hold the ball in place. The top piece will be held on with a screw.

Sizing the hole: How big is the hole? Good question. Let's assume the gap between the top and bottom pieces is ½" (13mm). We can use the Pythagorean theorem to figure out exactly how wide to make the hole.

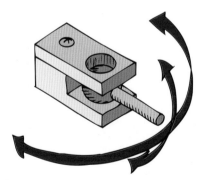

Clamping the joint: We don't have a drill bit the exact size needed for the hole, so let's make the hole a little smaller. This will allow the screw to firmly clamp the ball in position.

Ball-and-Socket Robot

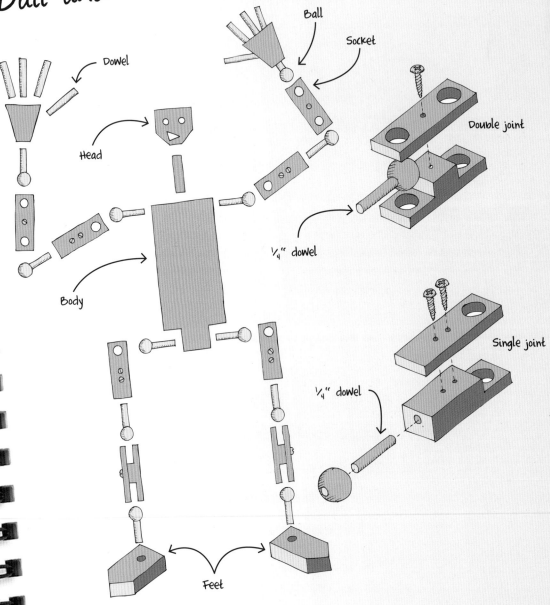

Dowel

Ball

Socket

Double joint

Head

¼" dowel

Body

¼" dowel

Single joint

Feet

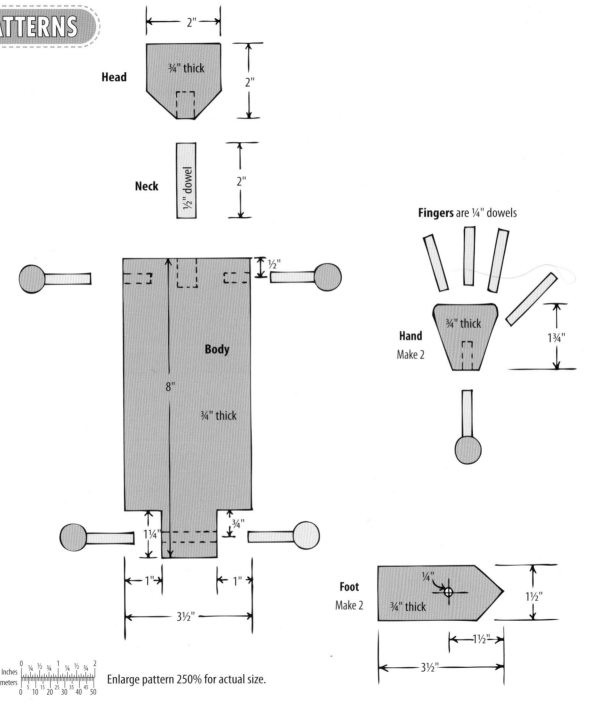

2"

Head

¾" thick

2"

Neck

½" dowel

2"

Fingers are ¼" dowels

Hand
Make 2

¾" thick

1¾"

Body

½"

8"

¾" thick

1¼"

¾"

1" 1"

3½"

Foot
Make 2

¼"

¾" thick

1½"

1½"

3½"

Inches
Millimeters

0 ¼ ½ ¾ 1 ¼ ½ ¾ 2

0 5 10 15 20 25 30 35 40 45 50

Enlarge pattern 250% for actual size.

Zany Wooden Toys that **Whiz, Spin, Pop,** and **Fly**

BALL-AND-SOCKET ROBOT

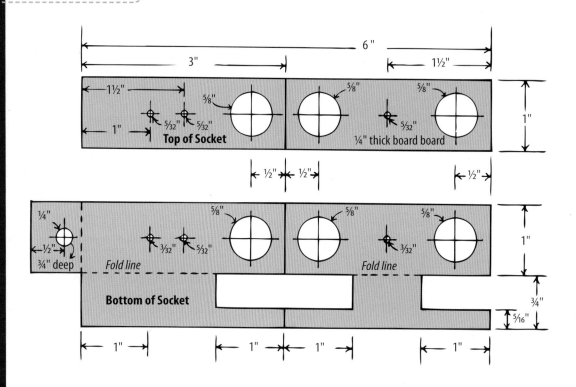

6 "

3"

1½"

1½"

5/8"

5/8"

5/8"

1"

5/32"

5/32"

Top of Socket

¼" thick board board

½"   ½"

½"

¼"

5/8"

5/8"

5/8"

1"

½"

3/32"

5/32"

3/32"

¾" deep

Fold line

Fold line

Bottom of Socket

¾"

5/16"

1"   1"   1"   1"

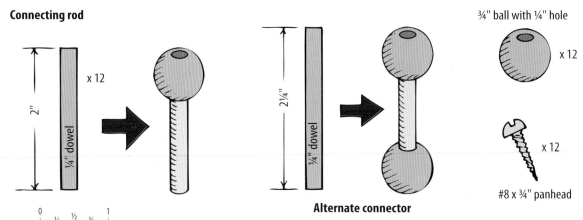

Connecting rod

x 12

2"

¼" dowel

2¼"

¼" dowel

Alternate connector

¾" ball with ¼" hole

x 12

x 12

#8 x ¾" panhead

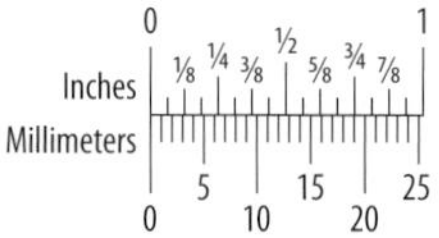

Inches
Millimeters

0   ⅛ ¼ ⅜ ½ ⅝ ¾ ⅞ 1

5   10   15   20   25

Enlarge pattern 135% for actual size.

*Zany Wooden Toys that **Whiz, Spin, Pop,** and **Fly***

MATERIALS & TOOLS

- ☑ ¾" (19mm) x 3½" (89mm) x 8" (203mm) pine board for body

- ☑ ¾" (19mm) x 2" (51mm) x 13" (330mm) pine board for head, hands, and feet

- ☑ ¾" (19mm) x 1" (25mm) x 25" (635mm) pine board for bottom pieces of sockets

- ☑ ¼" (6mm) x 1" (25mm) x 25" (635mm) pine board for top pieces of sockets

- ☑ ½" (13mm) dowel, 2" (51mm) long for neck

- ☑ ¼" (6mm) dowel, 36" (914mm) long for connecting rods, fingers, and face

- ☑ ¾" (19mm)-diameter wooden balls, 12

- ☑ #8 x ¾" (19mm) panhead screws, 12

- ☑ White or yellow glue

- ☑ Coping saw

- ☑ Miter saw

- ☑ Miter box

- ☑ Drill

- ☑ ³⁄₃₂" (2.5mm), ¼" (6mm), ½" (13mm), and ⅝" (16mm) drill bits

- ☑ Screwdriver to match screws

Engineering Advice:

Because there are so many joints to make, mass production can be very helpful. Start with pieces 12" (305mm) to 24" (610mm) long for the ¼" (6mm) x 1" (25mm) and ¾" (19mm) x 1" (25mm) boards. Mark the top of the ¼" (6mm) board and the side of the ¾" (19mm) board for as many pieces as possible. Drill all the screw holes in the ¼" (6mm) board. Next, attach the ¼" (6mm) board to the top of the ¾" (19mm) board by inserting a screw at each end. Drill the remaining ⅝" (16mm) holes. Mark pairs with unique hash marks, and cut each pair apart. Finish the cuts on the bottom pieces and then reassemble the matching pairs.

¼"

¾"

1"

Using screws as fasteners allows the joints to be loosened or tightened.

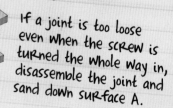

A

If a joint is too loose even when the screw is turned the whole way in, disassemble the joint and sand down surface A.

GUMBALL MACHINES

This section offers four fun interactive twists on the traditional gumball machine. The first design, the Kicker Treat Gumball Machine (page 164), requires skillful coordination to use a miniature wooden foot to kick a gumball through a dispensing hole. Next, it is up to you to free a gumball from the Poparazzi Gumball Machine (page 174) using only a mallet or the pushdown popper from Poparazzi Popper (page 181). The final project, the Monkey Toss Gumball Machine (page 186), offers your feet an opportunity to get involved—stomp on this machine to activate a gumball catapult. No matter which contraption you choose, you'll never think of gumballs in the same way again.

Kicker Treat
GUMBALL MACHINE

This project is fun to make but even more fun to decorate. I was so excited to finally get it working that I never thought of making it look nice. Then one day I got inspired to add color, shape, and whimsy to it—that ended up being just as much fun! So enjoy building this project, then enjoy getting gumballs from it, and then enjoy making it unique.

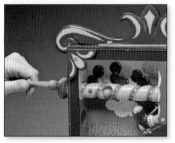

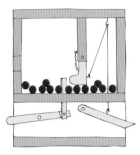

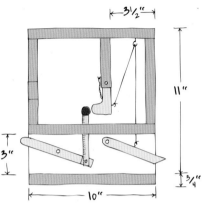

The basics: The gumball machine will be 10" (254mm) wide and 11¾" (298mm) tall (i.e., the width of a standard 1 x 12 board plus a ¾" [19mm] base). There will be a dowel connected to a lever for raising the gumball. There will be a lever for pulling back the foot and kicking the gumball. The foot will be mounted close to the center because it's the main attraction. That's one good idea—and here are some wrong turns and the final right one.

Wrong turn #1: I thought that if the gumball machine was partially filled with gumballs, then you could push a pedestal up through the gumballs and have one stay on top. Wrong! The gumballs either didn't align well enough or they were knocked off by other gumballs. I couldn't get a gumball to stay on the pedestal.

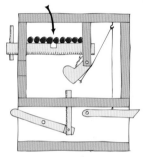

Wrong turn #2: Instead of a sea of gumballs, I decided to dispense one gumball at a time. I added a 1" (25mm) dowel with a ¾" (19mm) hole to dispense one gumball. Unfortunately, the gumballs aligned perfectly, but not directly above the hole, so I couldn't dispense any gumballs. I redesigned the machine so that the 1" (25mm) dowel could be moved left and right to capture a gumball.

Wrong turn #3 and final success: Okay, so now the gumball was dispensed, but it just sat there. I couldn't get it to roll over to the pedestal. I had to redo the bottom of the frame. Instead of a solid piece of wood, I screwed together two pieces that were ¾" (19mm) wide. After drilling the holes, I disassembled the pieces and sanded a trough toward the gumball pedestal. Finally, a gumball made it to the pedestal, was lifted up, got kicked by the foot, flew out the hole, and landed on the floor where I found it and ate it. Sweet success!

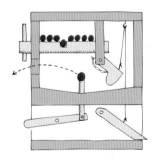

Kicker Treat Gumball Machine

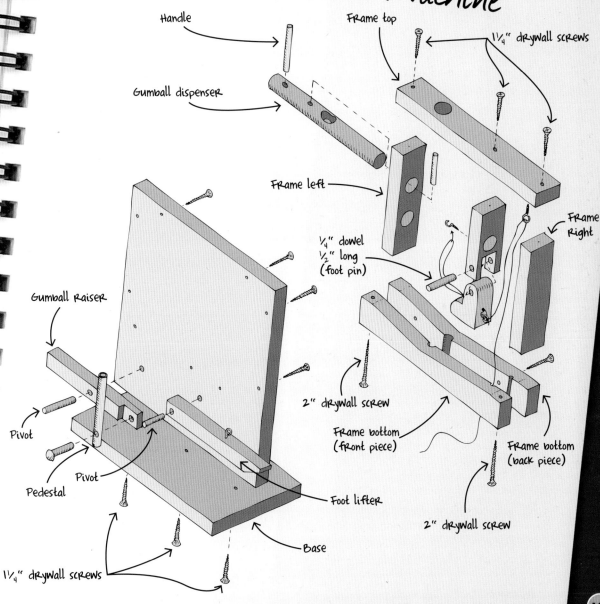

Handle

Frame top

1¼" drywall screws

Gumball dispenser

Frame left

¼" dowel
½" long
(foot pin)

Frame Right

Gumball Raiser

2" drywall screw

Frame bottom
(front piece)

Frame bottom
(back piece)

Pivot

Pedestal

Pivot

Foot lifter

2" drywall screw

Base

1¼" drywall screws

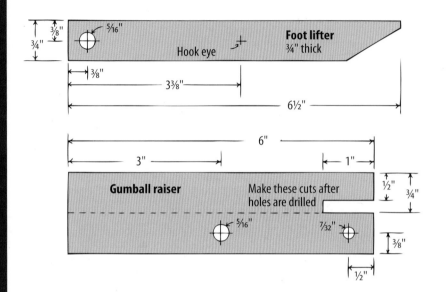

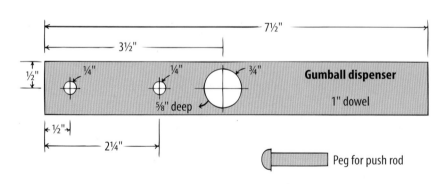

Hook eye

Foot lifter
¾" thick

Use a ⅜" drill bit to make a slight indentation on the end of the dowel

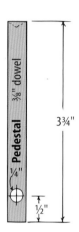

Pedestal ⅜" dowel

Gumball raiser

Make these cuts after holes are drilled

Gumball dispenser
1" dowel

⅝" deep

Peg for push rod

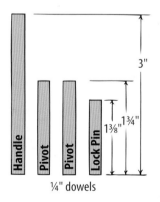

Handle

Pivot

Pivot

Lock Pin

¼" dowels

Inches
Millimeters

Enlarge pattern 180% for actual size.

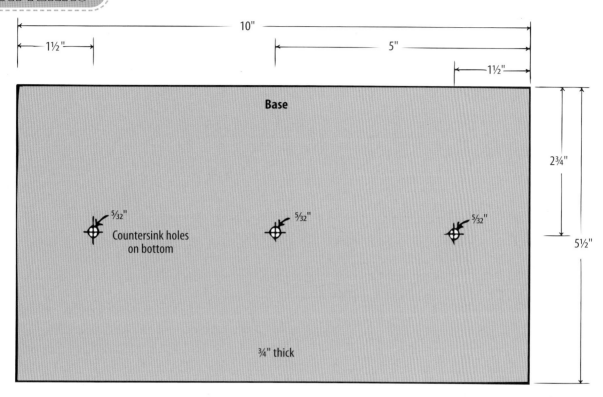

Base

10"

1½"

5"

1½"

2¾"

5½"

5/32"

5/32"

5/32"

Countersink holes
on bottom

¾" thick

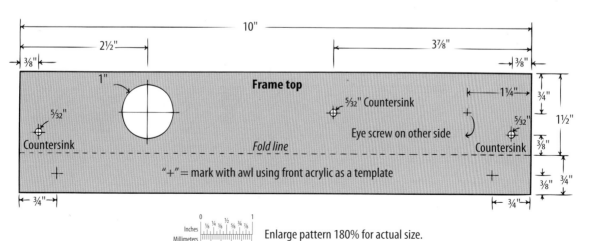

10"

2½"

3⅞"

⅜"

⅜"

1"

Frame top

5/32" Countersink

1¼"

¾"

5/32"

5/32"

Eye screw on other side

1½"

Countersink

Fold line

Countersink

⅜"

Countersink

⅜"

"+" = mark with awl using front acrylic as a template

¾"

¾"

¾"

0   1
Inches ⅛ ¼ ⅜ ½ ⅝ ¾ ⅞
Millimeters
0   5   10   15   20   25

Enlarge pattern 180% for actual size.

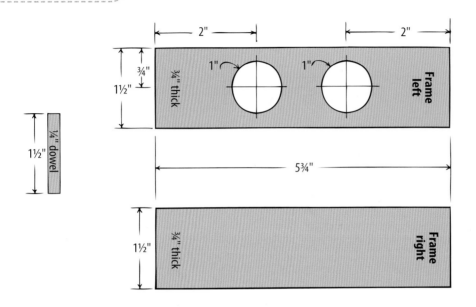

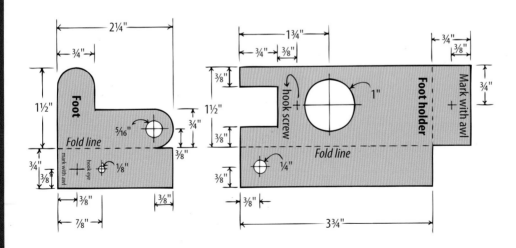

Enlarge pattern 180% for actual size.

KICKER TREAT GUMBALL MACHINE

Zany Wooden Toys that **Whiz, Spin, Pop,** *and* **Fly**

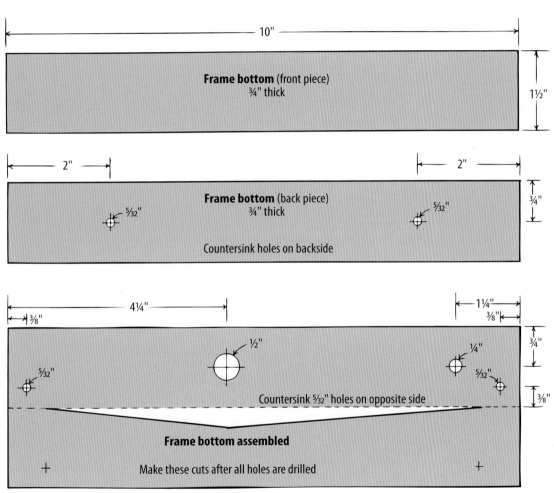

10"

Frame bottom (front piece)
¾" thick

1½"

2"   2"

Frame bottom (back piece)
¾" thick

⁵⁄₃₂"   ⁵⁄₃₂"

Countersink holes on backside

¾"

4¼"   1¼"
⅜"   ⅜"

½"   ¼"

⁵⁄₃₂"   ⁵⁄₃₂"

¾"

Countersink ⁵⁄₃₂" holes on opposite side

⅜"

Frame bottom assembled

+   Make these cuts after all holes are drilled   +

"+" = mark with awl using front acrylic as a template

Inches
Millimeters

Enlarge pattern 180% for actual size.

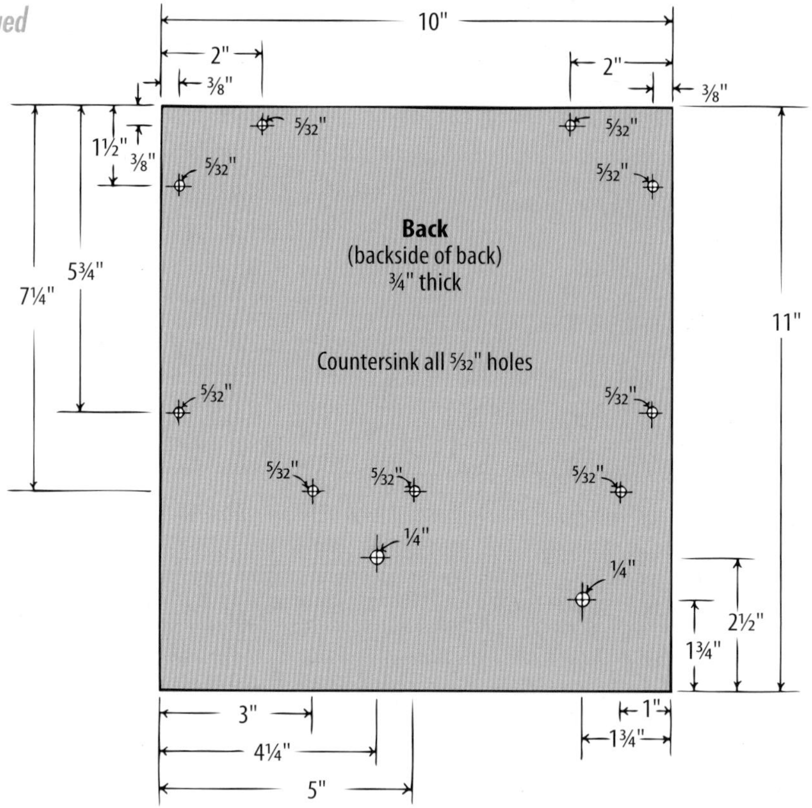
10"
2"
3⁄8"
2"
3⁄8"
11⁄2"
3⁄8"
5⁄32"
Back
(backside of back)
3⁄4" thick
Countersink all 5⁄32" holes
53⁄4"
71⁄4"
11"
1⁄4"
21⁄2"
13⁄4"
3"
41⁄4"
5"
1"
13⁄4"

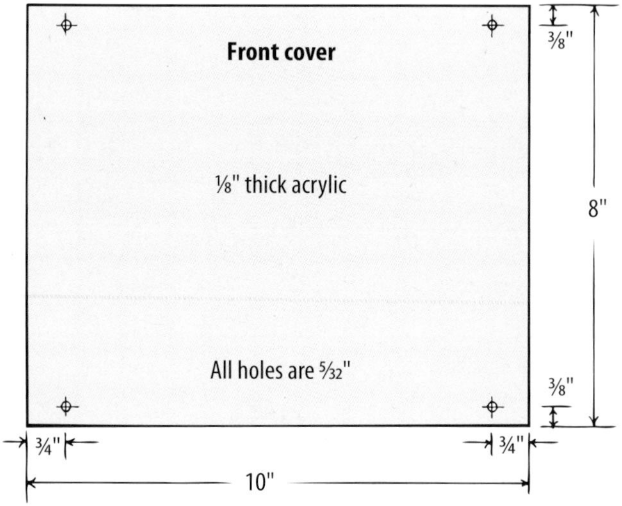
Front cover
1⁄8" thick acrylic
All holes are 5⁄32"
3⁄8"
8"
3⁄8"
3⁄4"
3⁄4"
10"

Inches / Millimeters

Enlarge pattern 365% for actual size.

- ☑ $\frac{3}{4}$" (19mm) x 10" (254mm) x 11" (279mm) pine board for back
- ☑ $\frac{3}{4}$" (19mm) x $5\frac{1}{2}$" (140mm) x 10" (254mm) pine board for base
- ☑ $\frac{3}{4}$" (19mm) x $1\frac{1}{2}$" (38mm) x 61" (1549mm) pine board for frame, foot lifter, foot, gumball raiser and foot holder
- ☑ 1" (25mm) dowel, $7\frac{1}{2}$" (191mm) long for gumball dispenser
- ☑ $\frac{3}{8}$" (10mm) dowel, $3\frac{3}{4}$" (95mm) long for pedestal
- ☑ $\frac{1}{4}$" (6mm) dowel, 10" (254mm) long for handle, pivots, and lock pin
- ☑ Peg
- ☑ $\frac{1}{8}$" (3mm) x 8" (203mm) x 10" (254mm) Acrylic for front cover
- ☑ $1\frac{1}{4}$" (32mm) drywall screws, 15
- ☑ 2" (51mm) drywall screws, 2
- ☑ #4 x $\frac{3}{4}$" (19mm) panhead screws for front, 4
- ☑ Eye screws, 3
- ☑ Hook screw
- ☑ 18" (457mm) nylon string
- ☑ #64 $3\frac{1}{2}$" (89mm) x $\frac{1}{4}$" (6mm) Rubber band
- ☑ Gumballs
- ☑ Coping saw
- ☑ Crosscut saw
- ☑ Miter saw
- ☑ Miter box

- ☑ Drill
- ☑ $\frac{1}{8}$" (3mm), $\frac{5}{32}$" (4mm), $\frac{7}{32}$" (5.5mm), $\frac{1}{4}$" (6mm), $\frac{5}{16}$" (8mm), $\frac{1}{2}$" (13mm), $\frac{3}{4}$" (19mm), and 1" (25mm) drill bits
- ☑ Countersink bit
- ☑ Screwdrivers (Phillips and standard)
- ☑ Needle-nose pliers for eye screws and hook screws
- ☑ Vise for holding small pieces
- ☑ Sandpaper for smoothing trough
- ☑ Thin wire for pulling rubber band

Engineering Advice:

When constructing the frame bottom, sand it to aid in guiding the gumballs to the proper spot. Sand a trough that tilts toward the hole from all four sides.

Poparazzi
GUMBALL MACHINE

This is not a toy! You thought it was, but it has evolved into something much bigger. Now, it is you versus the gumball. You thought you had superior intelligence and speed, but the gumball is anticipating your every move—it is smarter and quicker than you. Your frustration rises. Your concentration intensifies. You lock eyes with the gumball. You just need one well-aimed hit. Pop! The gumball flies through the air. You grab it with one hand and slam it into your mouth. "Piece of cake," you say aloud, while secretly hoping nobody notices the beads of sweat on your forehead.

Zany Wooden Toys that Whiz, Spin, Pop, and Fly

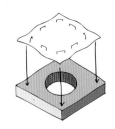

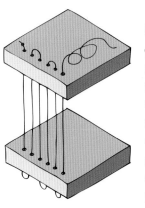

Popping the gumball: Let's do a little experiment. First, make a hammer by putting a 1" (25mm)-diameter wooden ball on the end of an 8" (203mm)-long piece of ¼" (6mm) dowel. Next, cut a 2" (51mm)-diameter hole in a piece of scrap wood. Stretch a piece of cloth over the back and staple or tack it in place. Flip the wood over, attach the piece to a base as shown, and put a gumball on the cloth. Use the hammer to hit the underside of the cloth. This works great! The gumball can go several feet high. Let's go with this idea.

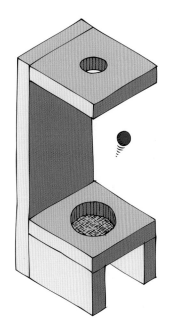

Containing the gumball: To keep the gumball from flying out sideways, we need to add walls. These walls should be transparent so we can see what we're doing. Plastic or screen walls would work but would take more time. Let's try building walls of string.

Getting the gumball: We need to add another challenge to the machine. If we're popping the gumball into the air, then we'll make a top with a hole above the gumball that the ball has to pass through.

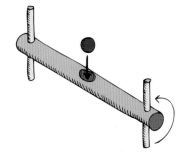

Dispensing the gumball: A gumball is about ⅝" (16mm) in diameter. A ¾" (19mm) hole in a 1" (25mm) dowel allows us to dispense one gumball at a time.

Poparazzi Gumball Machine

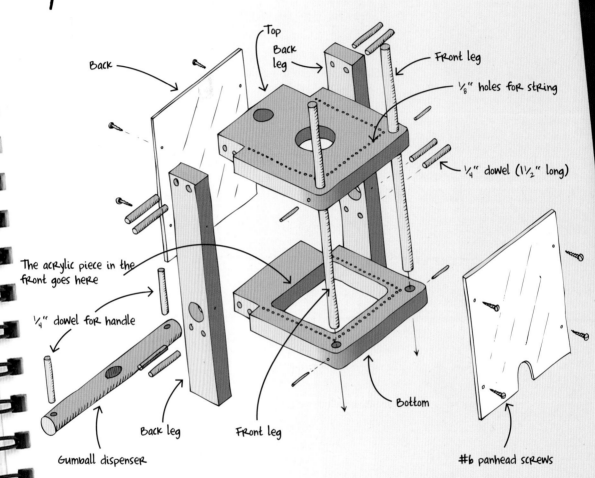

Back

Top

Back leg

Front leg

⅛" holes for string

¼" dowel (1½" long)

The acrylic piece in the front goes here

¼" dowel for handle

Back leg

Front leg

Gumball dispenser

Bottom

#6 panhead screws

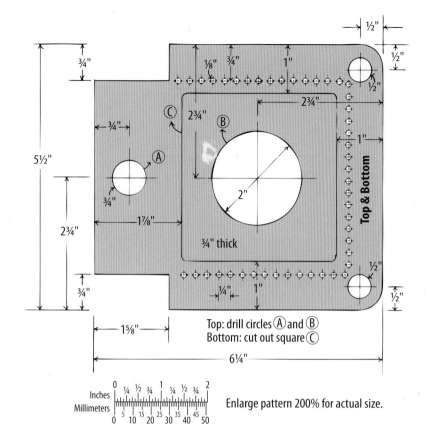

¾"
¾"
½"
½"
½"
⅛"
¾"
1"
2¾"
C
2¾"
B
A
¾"
5½"
2¾"
¾"
1⅞"
1"
2"
¾" thick
1"
½"
¼"
1"
½"

Top & Bottom

1⅝"

Top: drill circles Ⓐ and Ⓑ
Bottom: cut out square Ⓒ

6¼"

Inches
0 ¼ ½ ¾ 1 ¼ ½ ¾ 2
Millimeters
0 5 10 15 20 25 30 35 40 45 50

Enlarge pattern 200% for actual size.

If you ever see a gumball machine with a big plastic dome, flick the side with your finger. A gumball will pop up. Now you've made a gumball machine where you have to pop your gumball out...

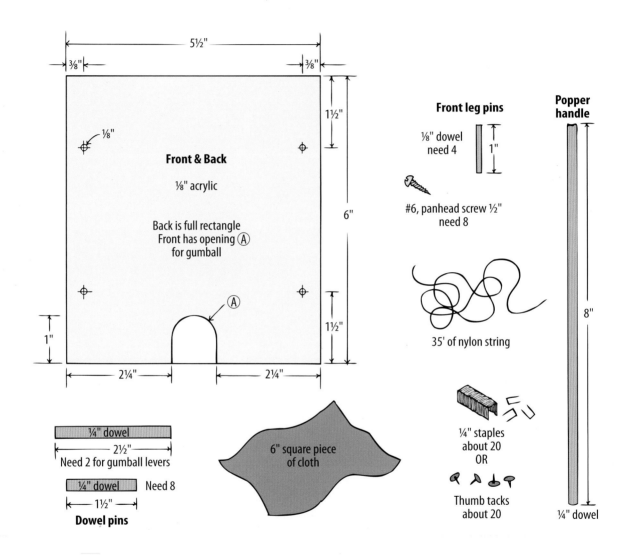

5½"

⅜"   ⅜"

⅛"

1½"

Front & Back

⅛" acrylic

Back is full rectangle
Front has opening Ⓐ
for gumball

6"

Ⓐ

1½"

1"

2¼"   2¼"

Front leg pins

⅛" dowel
need 4

1"

#6, panhead screw ½"
need 8

Popper handle

8"

¼" dowel

¼" dowel
2½"
Need 2 for gumball levers

¼" dowel   Need 8
1½"
Dowel pins

6" square piece
of cloth

35' of nylon string

¼" staples
about 20
OR

Thumb tacks
about 20

Inches
Millimeters

0 ¼ ½ ¾ 1 ¼ ½ ¾ 2

0 5 10 15 20 25 30 35 40 45 50

Enlarge pattern 200% for actual size.

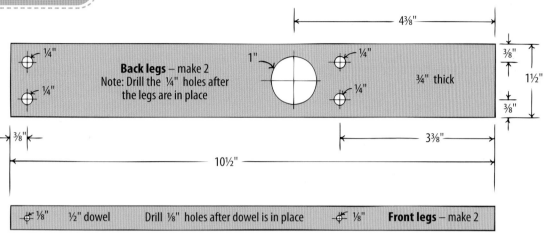

Back legs – make 2
Note: Drill the ¼" holes after the legs are in place

4⅜"
¼"
¼"
1"
¼"
¼"
¾" thick
⅜"
1½"
⅜"
⅜"
10½"
3⅜"

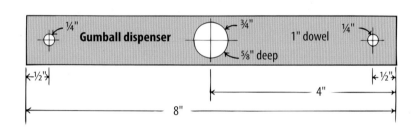

⅛"   ½" dowel   Drill ⅛" holes after dowel is in place   ⅛"   **Front legs** – make 2

Gumball dispenser
¼"   ¾"   1" dowel   ¼"
⅝" deep
½"   ½"
4"
8"

Inches
0 ¼ ½ ¾ 1 ¼ ½ ¾ 2
Millimeters
0 5 10 15 20 25 30 35 40 45 50

Enlarge pattern 200% for actual size.

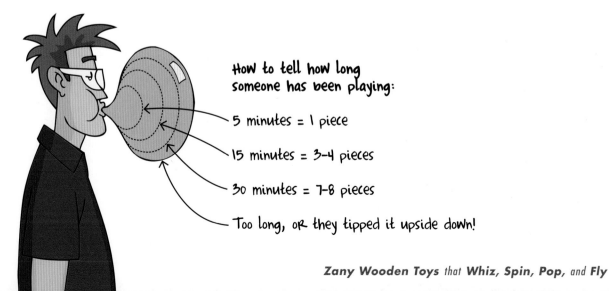

How to tell how long someone has been playing:

5 minutes = 1 piece

15 minutes = 3-4 pieces

30 minutes = 7-8 pieces

Too long, or they tipped it upside down!

- ☑ ³/₄" (19mm) x 5½" (140mm) x 13" (330mm) pine board for top and bottom
- ☑ ³/₄" (19mm) x 1½" (38mm) x 21" (533mm) pine board for back legs
- ☑ 1" (25mm) dowel, 8" (203mm) long for gumball dispenser
- ☑ ½" (13mm) dowel, 21" (533mm) long for front legs
- ☑ ¼" (6mm) dowel, 25" (635mm) long for popper handle, gumball levers, and dowel pins
- ☑ ⅛" (3mm) dowel, 4" (102mm) long for front leg pins
- ☑ 1" (25mm) wooden ball for popper
- ☑ ⅛" (3mm) x 5½" (140mm) x 6" (152mm) acrylic for front and back, 2
- ☑ #6 ½" (13mm) panhead screws, 8
- ☑ Staples or tacks, 20
- ☑ 6" (152mm) square of colorful fabric
- ☑ 35' (10,668mm) nylon string
- ☑ Gumballs
- ☑ Patience
- ☑ Coping saw
- ☑ Miter saw
- ☑ Miter box
- ☑ Drill
- ☑ ⅛" (3mm), ¼" (6mm), ½" (13mm), ³/₄" (19mm), and 1" (25mm) drill bits
- ☑ Hammer
- ☑ Vise for holding pieces
- ☑ Stapler (optional)
- ☑ Scissors
- ☑ Sandpaper

*Zany Wooden Toys that **Whiz**, **Spin**, **Pop**, and **Fly***

Engineering Advice:

By now, you're familiar with all the woodworking tools and techniques used in this project. Dowel pins are used to hold the base together instead of screws. The only new step is stretching the cloth. Choose somewhere to start by holding the cloth secure with a staple or tack. Always stretch it taut from the opposite side and it will look great.

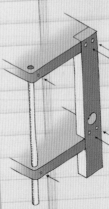

Cut two boards 5½" (140mm) x 6" (152mm) for the top and bottom pieces with the grain running from front to back. Screw them together with a 1½" (38mm) drywall screw in the center. Now make the cuts for the back legs. Next, drill the ½" (13mm) holes for the front legs and all the ⅛" (3mm) holes for the string wall. Doing this ensures both parts are identical.

Drill the holes for the dowel pins with the legs in place. The ¼" (6mm) holes for the back legs are 1½" (38mm) deep. The ⅛" (3mm) holes for the front legs are 1" (25mm) deep.

Poparazzi
POPPER

This is a companion toy to the Poparazzi Gumball Machine (page 174). The popper makes it a little easier for younger children to pop out a gumball.

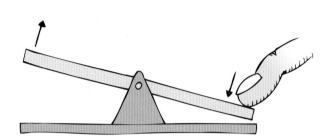

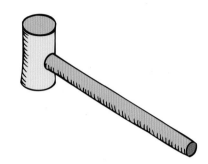

The contraption: When a kid pushes down, we want a hammer to go up to hit the gumball. Finger down—hammer up. Down-up-down-up. Sounds like a teeter-totter to me.

Popping the gumball: A flat-ended hammer would give more accuracy than the round ball hammer we made for the Poparazzi Gumball Machine. Use a piece of ½" (13mm) dowel for the popper's head.

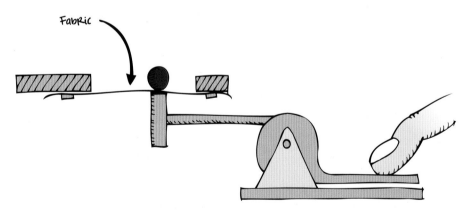

Fabric

Sizing the popper: How big? The popper handle should reach to the far end of the fabric-covered hole and still allow a kid enough space to push down on the seesaw. Also, the popper should only go up about ¼" (6mm) higher than the cloth. We don't want too much force on the fabric.

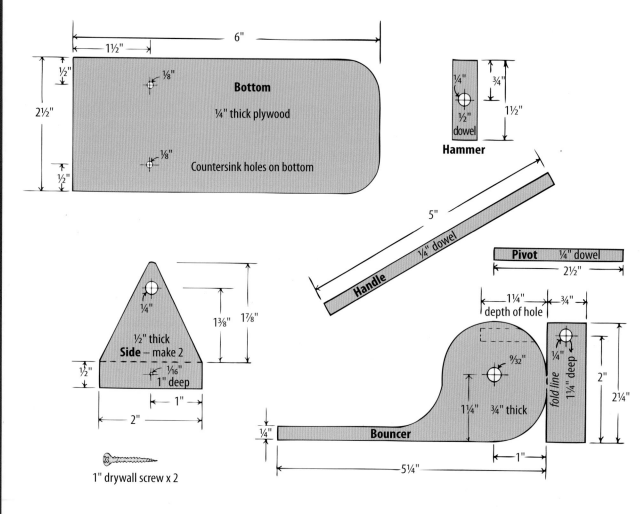

Bottom

¼" thick plywood

Countersink holes on bottom

⅛"

⅛"

6"

1½"

½"

2½"

½"

Hammer

¼"

½" dowel

¾"

1½"

Handle

¼" dowel

5"

Pivot   ¼" dowel

2½"

Side – make 2

½" thick

¼"

1⅜"

1⅞"

½"

1/16"

1" deep

1"

2"

Bouncer

¾" thick

1¼"

9/32"

1¼"
depth of hole

¾"

fold line

1¼" deep

¼"

2"

2¼"

¼"

1"

5¼"

1" drywall screw x 2

Inches
Millimeters

Enlarge pattern 180% for actual size.

Zany Wooden Toys that *Whiz, Spin, Pop,* and *Fly*

☑ ¾" (19mm) x 2¼" (57mm) x 5¼" (133mm) pine board for bouncer

☑ ½" (13mm) x 1⅞" (48mm) x 4" (102mm) pine board for sides

☑ ¼" (6mm) x 2½" (64mm) x 6" (152mm) plywood for bottom

☑ ½" (13mm) dowel, 1½" (38mm) long for hammer

☑ ¼" (6mm) dowel, 8" (203mm) long for handle and pivot

☑ Dowel caps, 2 (optional)

☑ 1" (25mm) drywall screws, 2

☑ Coping saw

☑ Drill

☑ 1/16" (2mm), ⅛" (3mm), ¼" (6mm), and 9/32" (7mm) drill bits

☑ Screwdriver to match screws

Engineering Advice:

I have rounded the side of the hammer that rests on the ground so that the force of using the popper doesn't chip the edges. (Actually, I rounded it so that the head could be twisted around to make gumball retrieval harder for the next guy!)

If you wish, you could use graphite on the dowel and bouncer. Be sure to sand any dry paint from the inside of the hole in the bouncer, and the popper should operate smoothly.

To make the Poparazzi Gumball Machine mentioned here, follow the instructions on pages 174-180.

*Zany Wooden Toys that **Whiz, Spin, Pop,** and **Fly***

Monkey Toss
GUMBALL MACHINE

This is by far the most challenging toy we'll make, but believe me, this gumball machine decorated to look like a monkey is worth the extra effort and the bit of trial and error involved. You will have a line of kids and adults waiting to try it out. Here's what most people do:

- First gumball goes only about 6" high because they are a little timid on the stomp.

- Second gumball bounces off the ceiling due to over-correction of the stomp.

- Third gumball is delivered right to the hand and they grin from ear-to-ear.

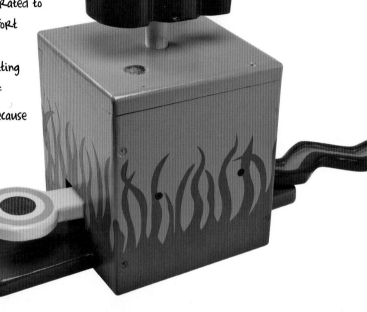

Zany Wooden Toys that **Whiz, Spin, Pop,** and **Fly**

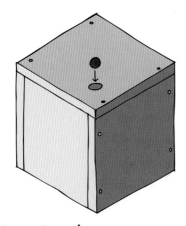

Sits on the floor: Easy enough—start with a square box full of gumballs.

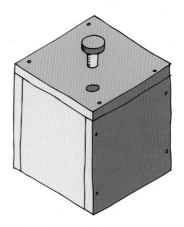

Operated by foot: Stepping on a large, sturdy button dispenses a gumball—but to where?

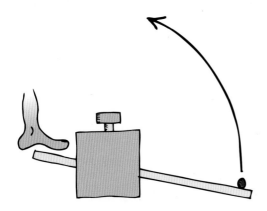

Delivers the gumball: If the gumball rolled down to the end of a teeter-totter, then you could stomp on the other side to fling the gumball into your hand.

Fun in the making: Make sure you test out the different pieces as you make them. If something doesn't work quite right, then enjoy the troubleshooting and mental exercise required for fixing it. And have fun with the button. Draw a monkey face on it or whatever else you want—maybe even put a picture of yourself on it.

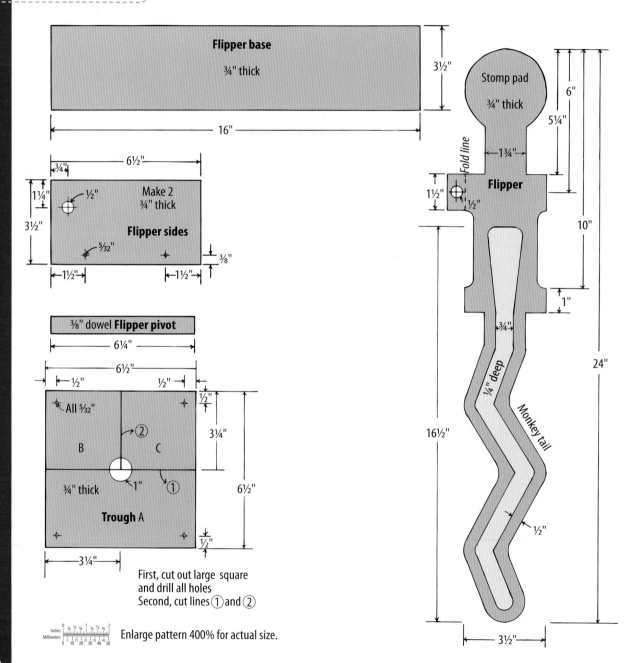

Flipper base

¾" thick

3½"

16"

6½"

¾"

1¼"

½"

Make 2
¾" thick

Flipper sides

3½"

5/32"

3/8"

1½"

1½"

⅜" dowel **Flipper pivot**

6¼"

6½"

½"

½"

All 5/32"

½"

②

3¼"

B

C

¾" thick

1"

①

6½"

Trough A

½"

3¼"

First, cut out large square
and drill all holes
Second, cut lines ① and ②

Inches
Millimeters

0 ¼ ½ ¾ 1 1¼ 1½ 1¾ 2
0 5 10 15 20 25 30 35 40 45 50

Enlarge pattern 400% for actual size.

Stomp pad

¾" thick

6"

5¼"

Fold line

1¾"

Flipper

1½"

½"

10"

1"

¾"

¼" deep

Monkey tail

16½"

½"

24"

3½"

MONKEY TOSS GUMBALL MACHINE

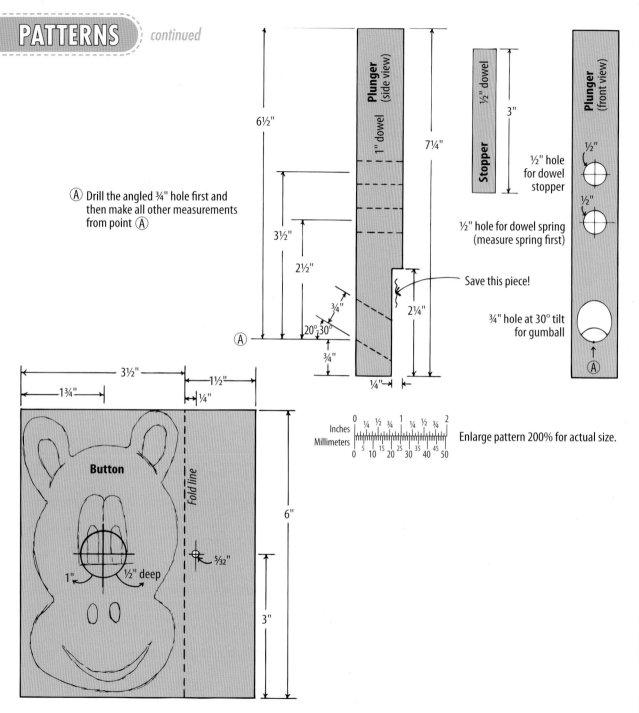

Ⓐ Drill the angled ¾" hole first and then make all other measurements from point Ⓐ

Plunger (side view)

6½"

7¼"

1" dowel

3½"

2½"

2¼"

¾"

20° 30°

¾"

¼"

Ⓐ

Stopper

½" dowel

3"

½" hole for dowel stopper

½" hole for dowel spring (measure spring first)

Save this piece!

¾" hole at 30° tilt for gumball

Plunger (front view)

½"

½"

Ⓐ

3½"

1¾"

1½"

¼"

Button

Fold line

6"

3"

1"

½" deep

5⁄32"

Inches 0 ¼ ½ ¾ 1 ¼ ½ ¾ 2
Millimeters 0 5 10 15 20 25 30 35 40 45 50

Enlarge pattern 200% for actual size.

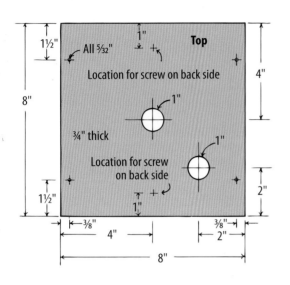

Top

1½"

All 5⁄32"

Location for screw on back side

¾" thick

Location for screw on back side

8"

4"

2"

1½"

1"

1"

1"

⅜"

4"

⅜"

2"

8"

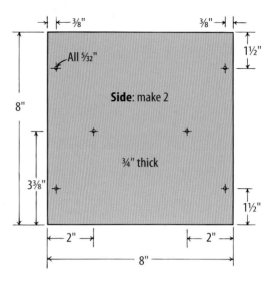

⅜"

⅜"

1½"

All 5⁄32"

Side: make 2

¾" thick

8"

3⅜"

1½"

2"

2"

8"

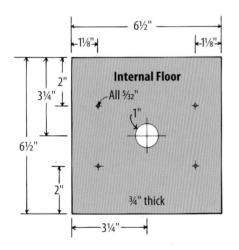

6½"

1⅛"

1⅛"

Internal Floor

All 5⁄32"

2"

3¼"

1"

6½"

2"

¾" thick

3¼"

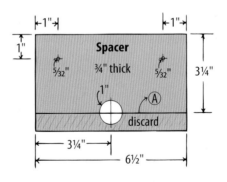

1"

1"

1"

Spacer

5⁄32"

¾" thick

5⁄32"

3¼"

1"

discard

A

3¼"

6½"

Cut out piece 6½" x 4" and drill holes. Next, cut along line and discard the small piece (shaded area).

Inches

Millimeters

Enlarge pattern 400% for actual size.

Zany Wooden Toys that Whiz, Spin, Pop, and Fly

MONKEY TOSS GUMBALL MACHINE

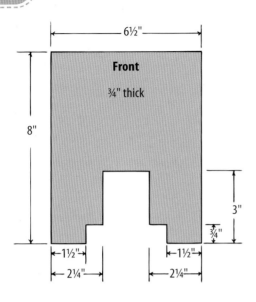

6½"

Front

¾" thick

8"

3"

¾"

1½" 1½"

2¼" 2¼"

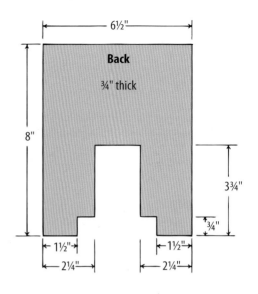

6½"

Back

¾" thick

8"

3¾"

¾"

1½" 1½"

2¼" 2¼"

Inches
Millimeters

Enlarge pattern 400% for actual size.

Traditional gumball machines are designed to be operated by your hands. Thus, they are waist-high and you have to twist a handle with one hand and catch the gumball with the other. I think a gumball machine that sits on the floor, is operated only by your feet, and delivers a gumball directly to your hand is way more fun!

MONKEY TOSS GUMBALL MACHINE

Zany Wooden Toys that **Whiz, Spin, Pop, and Fly**

- ☑ ¾" (19mm) x 8" (203mm) x 8" (203mm) pine board for top and sides, 3

- ☑ ¾" (19mm) x 6½" (165mm) x 8" (203mm) pine board for front and back, 2

- ☑ ¾" (19mm) x 6½" (165mm) x 6½" (165mm) pine board for internal floor, spacer, and trough, 3

- ☑ ¾" (19mm) x 3½" (89mm) x 16" (406mm) pine board for flipper base

- ☑ ¾" (19mm) x 3½" (89mm) x 6½" (165mm) pine board for flipper sides, 2

- ☑ ¾" (19mm) x 3½" (89mm) x 24" (610mm) pine board for flipper (stomp pad and tail)

- ☑ 1½" (38mm) x 3½" (89mm) x 6" (152mm) pine board for button (monkey face)

- ☑ 1" (25mm) dowel, 7¼" (184mm) long for plunger

- ☑ ½" (13mm) dowel, 3" (76mm) long for stopper

- ☑ ⅜" (10mm) dowel, 6¼" (159mm) long for flipper pivot

- ☑ ¹⁵⁄₃₂" (12mm) x 4½" (114mm) x .041" (1mm) spring (use whatever you can find)

- ☑ #8 or #10 x ¾" (19mm) flathead screws, 2

- ☑ 1¼" (32mm) drywall screws, 30

- ☑ 2" (51mm) drywall screw

- ☑ White or yellow glue

- ☑ Gumballs galore

- ☑ Coping saw

- ☑ Crosscut saw

- ☑ Miter saw

- ☑ Miter box

- ☑ Drill

- ☑ ⁵⁄₃₂" (4mm), ¼" (6mm), ⅜" (10mm), ⁷⁄₁₆" (11mm), ½" (13mm), ¾" (19mm), and 1" (25mm) drill bits

- ☑ Router with ¾" (19mm)-wide square bit

- ☑ Vise

- ☑ Screwdriver to match screws

- ☑ File, rasp, or sandpaper

Fellow toy inventors:
By now, you are very skilled and exceedingly creative. You think outside the box, in 3-D, and upside down. I leave this project in good hands. It requires a lot of engineering along the way. When the instructions here are fuzzy or downright stink, I'm sure you'll figure it out. Live your life, protect your brain, and enjoy everything!

MONKEY TOSS GUMBALL MACHINE

Engineering Advice:

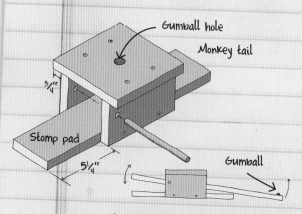

Gumball hole

Monkey tail

3/4"

Stomp pad

5 1/4"

Gumball

Assemble the trough and sides as shown. For clarity, the right side and the seesaw are not shown here.

Glue a 3/4" (19mm)-long waste section from the flat cut on the plunger to the backside of the hole at the base of the trough to prevent two gumballs from entering the plunger hole at the same time.

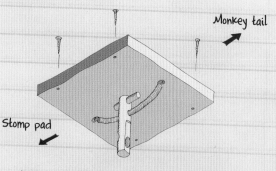

Assemble the base as shown. Insert the monkey tail lever from the left. Align the dowel holes and insert the 3/8" (10mm) dowel through the box and the tail. Try out the flipping action!

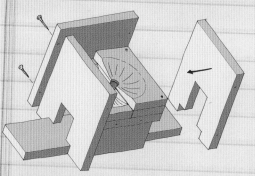

Monkey tail

Stomp pad

Sand down the trough so the gumballs roll to the middle. Attach each piece of the trough with a 1 1/4" (32mm) drywall screw. For clarity, the seesaw is not shown here.

The spring is attached with #8 or #10 x 3/4" (19mm) flathead screws. The top is attached to the base assembly using 1 1/4" (32mm) wood screws. The monkey face button is attached using a 2" (51mm) drywall screw to complete the project.

Appendix:
WOODWORKING BASICS

The toys in this notebook are primarily made out of wood. Why wood? The main reason is that wood is an ideal material for inventors. It's easy to find, easy to work with, fairly strong, and inexpensive. You can cut it, shape it, connect it, and decorate it with basic tools. You can also put in a little more time sanding and finishing the project and end up with a beautiful work of art.

The woodworking instructions in this book are geared toward providing the basics so that your ideas can take shape. There are many great books on woodworking that show the finer points of choosing wood, using tools, making precise joints, and creating fine finishes. For now, we're interested in capturing the prototype in wood just to see if it works. If we like it, then we'll make another one and take more time to make it a work of art.

SELECTING WOOD

Wood is a wonderful building material because it is strong, easy to work with, and easy to find. You need to know just a little about wood so you can walk into a hardware store with confidence and quickly get all the supplies you need to start work on your inventions.

Boards

All of the toys in this book were originally made with basic, construction-grade pine boards or plywood. This wood is readily available at hardware stores and lumberyards and comes in standard sizes. Make your first toys with inexpensive but good wood. You can always experiment with more interesting varieties later.

Sizes

Wood is sold in standard dimensions. The toys in this book were designed around these standard dimensions whenever possible to avoid having to make extra cuts. However, these dimensions can be a little deceiving when you're buying wood.

The wood is sold by the dimensions from which it was originally cut from the tree, such as 2" (51mm) thick by 4" (102mm) wide by so many feet long. The large saw used to make these cuts leaves a very rough, splintery surface on the boards. Luckily, the sawmill is kind enough to plane the boards smooth so woodworkers don't spend too much time removing splinters. The drawback is that the 2" (51mm) x 4" (102mm) board is now only 1½" (38mm) x 3½" (89mm). The sawmill took off ¼" (6mm) on each side. However, the board is still called a "two by four." For thinner boards, the sawmill takes off less. So, for example, a 1" (25mm) x 6" (152mm) board ends up being ¾" (19mm) x 5½" (140mm).

What this really means is that the more you work with wood, the better you become with fractions. The supply lists in this book call out the actual dimensions.

Construction-grade pine is a good choice for the projects in this book.

Zany Wooden Toys that Whiz, Spin, Pop, and Fly

How to choose good wood

Choosing good wood is not difficult, but there are a few things you'll want to watch for.

- **Warp:** Make sure the board lies flat on the floor and doesn't bend up or bend sideways. Look down the length of the board to ensure that it is straight.

- **Cracks:** Look at the ends of the boards to see if there are cracks. Cracks will be weak spots in your project.

- **Knots:** Knots are the dark circles that you see on most boards. They look nice, but they are very, very hard. Thus, they are difficult to nail, drill, and saw. Choose wood with few knots, and lay out your patterns to avoid them.

- **Other damage:** Boards can often have rough areas, scratches, or paint on them. You won't want to use that wood for your projects, so try to find boards that are as clean as possible.

Damaged and knotty boards will make construction difficult.

NOMINAL BOARD SIZE VS. ACTUAL SIZE		
Board Size	Actual Size	Lingo
1" (25mm) x 2" (51mm)	¾" (19mm) x 1½" (38mm)	one by two
1" (25mm) x 4" (102mm)	¾" (19mm) x 3½" (89mm)	one by four
1" (25mm) x 6" (152mm)	¾" (19mm) x 5½" (140mm)	one by six
1" (25mm) x 8" (203mm)	¾" (19mm) x 7½" (191mm)	one by eight
1" (25mm) x 12" (305mm)	¾" (19mm) x 11" (279mm)	one by twelve
2" (51mm) x 4" (102mm)	1½" (38mm) x 3½" (89mm)	two by four
2" (51mm) x 6" (152mm)	1½" (38mm) x 5½" (140mm)	two by six

Wood grain

The grain of the wood is the pattern of lines that you see in it. The grain lines run up and down the trunk of the tree and up and down the length of a pine board. The grain is important for two reasons: 1) looks and 2) strength. For now, we care only about strength.

Boards are stronger in the direction of the grain and weaker across the grain. To demonstrate this, cut about ¼" (6mm) off the end of a 1 x 4 board. Cut a similar size piece along the length of the board. Now, try to break the pieces. The board with end grain will snap very easily. The section cut with the long grain will be very difficult to break. This is important when laying out toys. Avoid using end grain on small pieces. When this is unavoidable, lay out the piece at a 45° angle to the grain.

End grain can be seen on the end of a board.

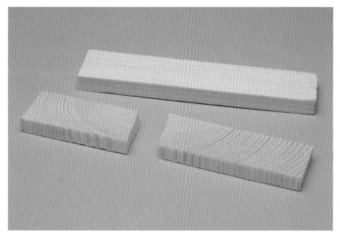
End-grain pieces break easily, but the section cut with the grain is strong.

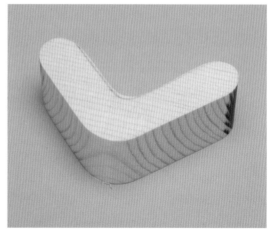
If you must cut a piece from end grain, lay out the piece at a 45° angle to the grain.

Plywood

Plywood is made by gluing thin layers of wood together. Each layer is placed with the grain perpendicular to the layer below. This creates a very strong, flat board. This strength is important for thin pieces (⅛" [3mm] and ¼" [6mm] thick) and for small pieces. Plywood comes in different quality grades, depending on the type of wood used, how smooth the surface is, and the type of glue used. Inexpensive plywood will work just fine for the projects in this book.

Dowels

Dowels are great! They are truly indispensable. They serve as axles, hinge pins, ramrods, and anchors for rubber bands. Dowels come in a variety of diameters and lengths. The projects in this book use dowels with ⅛" (3mm), ¼" (6mm), ⅜" (10mm), ½" (13mm), ¾" (19mm), and 1" (25mm) diameters. The diameters of dowels can be fairly unpredictable. Due to machining, they are not always perfectly round, and some will fit loosely in the hole while others will be too tight. For loose dowels, just wrap the dowel with a piece of tape or add a splinter of wood into the hole. For tight dowels, sanding will work.

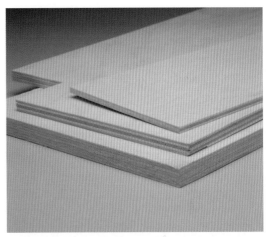

Plywood is made by gluing many layers of wood together, with each layer perpendicular to those on both sides of it.

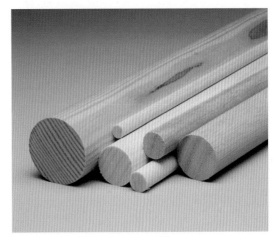

Dowels are available in a variety of diameters.

MAKING CUTS

Few projects can be made with full-length boards. Thus, you're going to have to learn how to cut boards down to size and how to shape them the way you want.

Straight cuts

If you need to cut a straight line, you'll want to use a handsaw. Handsaws are specifically designed for making straight cuts. A handsaw blade is wide and stiff, which makes it very easy to follow a straight line.

There are many types of handsaws in different sizes. For the projects in this book, you only need to be concerned about two things: 1) how many teeth per inch on the blade and 2) the length of the blade. The more teeth per inch a saw has, the cleaner the cut will be. A saw with 7 to 10 teeth per inch (TPI) will work fine. Saws come in sizes of about 12" (305mm), 15" (381mm), 20" (508mm), and 26" (660mm). Since the projects in this book are small, a 12" (305mm) or 15" (381mm) saw will be fine. Larger saws may be awkward to use on small pieces.

Miter Saw and Miter Box

A miter saw and miter box work together to help improve the accuracy of your straight cuts.

The miter box acts as a guide for the miter saw so you don't have to worry about keeping the blade straight. The simplest miter boxes are made out of plastic or wood. There are grooves in the miter box to hold the saw at set angles of 90°, 45°, and other angles. Follow the same steps as you would for using a handsaw. Remember to clamp your wood in the miter box, because small pieces are difficult to hold steady. You'll need a miter box for the Ultimate Adventurer's Vehicle (page 124).

Handsaws come in a variety of saw tooth sizes and teeth per inch.

*Zany Wooden Toys that **Whiz, Spin, Pop,** and **Fly***

HOW TO MAKE A STRAIGHT CUT

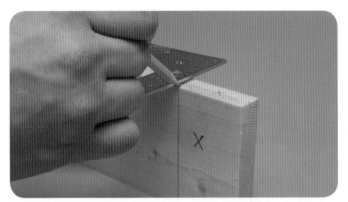

1 Mark your cutline on the top and side of the board to ensure the cut starts out at the correct angle. You will be cutting right next to the lines you marked. If you were to cut directly on the lines, your piece would end up slightly smaller than you intended due to the wood removed by the saw (also known as the saw kerf). I always put a small "X" on the side of the line that will be the waste, as a reminder of where to place the saw.

2 Clamp the wood so that the cutline is vertical. Make sure there's enough room for the saw. It is a good idea to put scrap wood between the clamp and the project piece to prevent any squashing.

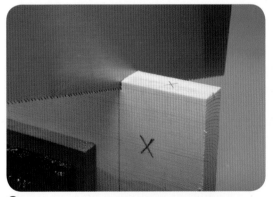

3 Start the cut by placing the back of the blade (i.e., the part nearest the handle) next to the pencil line on the corner farthest from your hand. Tilt the saw slightly downward. Your arm should line up with the line on the wood. Slowly pull back the saw. This will start the cut at the corner and leave a small groove. Repeat this several times to ensure that the saw is following your marks.

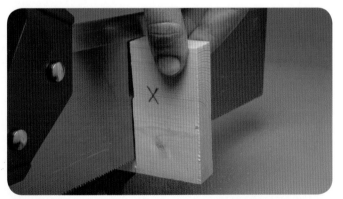

4 After a few backstrokes, start sawing with a slow back-and-forth motion. Make long, even strokes. Finish the cut by slowing down and using less downward pressure when you have about ¼" (6mm) left to go. Support the waste portion of the board with your free hand to prevent it from breaking loose and tearing out a splinter.

Zany Wooden Toys that Whiz, Spin, Pop, and Fly

Rabbets

"Rabbet" is just woodworking language for a channel or groove that is cut in the end of a board. It is made with two straight cuts. One cut is across the grain, and the other is on the end grain. You'll have to make a rabbet for the Rapid-Fire Nickel Launcher (page 70).

HOW TO MAKE A RABBET

1 Mark the width and depth of the rabbet on the top, end, and sides of the board. There will be six lines.

2 Clamp the board to a horizontal surface. Use your handsaw to cut down across the grain to the first mark. Make sure the saw hits the marks on the front and back edges.

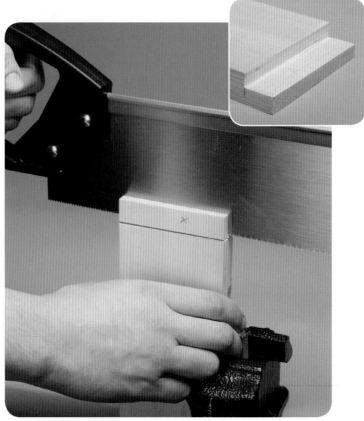

3 Reclamp your board so that the end grain is facing upward. Make the second cut on the end grain to complete the rabbet. The channel can be cleaned up with a chisel if need be.

Cutting with a coping saw

Use a coping saw for making curved cuts. It has a narrow, flexible blade that can change direction easily. The narrower the blade is, the tighter the curve it can cut. Coping saws cut on the pull stroke to prevent the blade from bending or buckling. Each end of the blade is connected to a pin that can rotate in the frame. This gives you much more freedom when cutting larger pieces. Just remember that the pins should always point in the same direction.

You can remove or replace the blade in a coping saw by turning the handle counterclockwise with respect to the frame. This will loosen the blade so that you can remove one or both ends.

Coping saws are used to cut curved lines.

HOW TO MAKE A CURVED CUT

1 Clamp your marked work piece vertically in a vise. Thin pieces tend to vibrate, so clamp as near to the cut as possible.

2 Start the cut by laying the blade flat against the cutline. Use several backstrokes to start the cut.

3 Control the cut by placing your index finger on the coping saw's frame. Keep the blade perpendicular to the face of the wood so that the saw pattern on the back is the same as on the front. Rotate the frame as needed to finish the cut.

4 Rotate the blade to prevent the frame from hitting the wood when making deep cuts.

HOW TO MAKE A SQUARE CUT

Use the coping saw to remove square pieces of wood. This requires four different cuts.

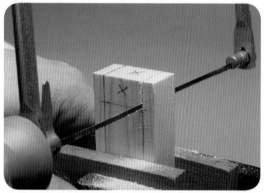

1 Cut down the right side.

2 Cut down the left side.

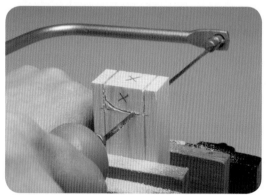

3 Back the saw a short distance out of the second cut, and create a curved cut that meets up with the bottom of the first cut.

4 Starting at the bottom of the first cut, saw horizontally back to the bottom of the second cut.

Zany Wooden Toys that *Whiz, Spin, Pop,* and *Fly*

HOW TO MAKE AN INTERNAL CUT

Use the coping saw for making internal cuts.
These are cuts that are surrounded by wood.

1 Drill a hole (see Drilling Holes, page 206) in the internal waste portion of the board wide enough for the end of the coping saw blade. Clamp the board in a vise.

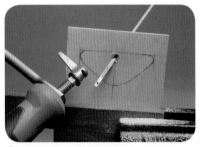

2 Detach one end of the blade from the coping saw frame by unscrewing the handle. Insert the blade into the hole in the work piece, and then reattach it to the frame.

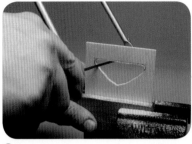

3 Complete the cut, and then detach and remove the blade.

Cutting plastic

Some of the gumball machine projects in this book require cutting clear plastic (acrylic) sheets for use as covers for the machines. Plastic can be cut and drilled with the same tools used for wood. Cutting plastic sheets requires a saw with very fine teeth, such as a coping saw. Support the plastic very near the cutline to prevent breaking it. Drill with a normal twist drill. Use a slow speed to prevent the plastic from heating and melting.

DRILLING HOLES

Round holes are a toymaker's friend. They form an important part of axles, hinges, and latches. The best part about holes is that they are very easy to make.

Drills

Hand drills—the human-powered ones—are fun to use, and there's a great sense of accomplishment with each hole made. However, I highly recommend using a very basic corded or cordless power drill. I find that I'm much more accurate when I'm free to concentrate on aligning the bit straight up and down.

The basic power drill has two parts of interest: 1) the trigger and 2) the chuck. Power drills have a pistol-style handle that allows you to drill holes with one hand. Your index finger activates the trigger—a gentle squeeze will start the drill. The chuck holds the different bits used for making holes. Get a drill with a chuck that can open up to ⅜" (10mm).

Hand drills are powered by muscle.

Cordless power drills allow you to focus on drilling a straight hole.

*Zany Wooden Toys that **Whiz, Spin, Pop,** and **Fly***

Drill bits

There are many different kinds of bits, and almost all sizes are available. Buy a set of 15 to 20 drill bits ranging from 1/6" (4mm) to ½" (13mm). The larger bits should have shanks no larger than ⅜" (10mm) to fit into your chuck.

Twist bits: Their spiral, or twisted, shape allows these bits to easily cut through wood, plastic, and metal. Twist drill bits are the most basic type of bit.

Brad tip bits: Also known as dowel bits, brad tip bits have a sharp point that prevents the bit from wandering when drilling into grainy or curved surfaces.

Forstner bits: These bits excel at cutting clean holes and are good for holes that enter the wood at an angle.

Spade bits: Chisel bits come in larger diameters but tend to tear the wood when exiting.

Hole-cutting bits: These are useful for very large holes.

Countersink bits: A countersink bit is also good to have. It creates a conical-shaped depression around an already drilled hole. This is needed to recess screw heads below the surface of the wood. A countersink bit is used just like a regular drill bit, but you apply just enough pressure to make an indentation the size of the screw you are using.

Helpful Hints for Drilling

Put a piece of masking tape on the drill when you need to drill holes to a certain depth.

Prevent splintering around the exit hole of your work piece by drilling onto a piece of scrap wood. With practice, you'll be able to feel when you've drilled through the top piece.

Make the exit hole cleaner by drilling the hole just deep enough for the center of the bit to poke through the other side. Flip the board over, and start drilling where the bit poked through.

There are many types of drill bits, including Forstner (left), brad tip (middle left), twist (middle), countersink (bottom), hole-cutting (right top), and chisel (right).

HOW TO DRILL A HOLE

1 Mark the location for the hole with an awl. This small indentation will prevent the bit from wandering away from the hole.

2 Clamp the wood in a vise so that the hole can be drilled with the bit straight up and down.

3 Align the bit so it is perpendicular to the work surface. The bit should be resting on the mark from the awl.

4 Squeeze the trigger to start drilling. Apply minimal downward force— the weight of the drill should be enough. Clear the sawdust out of the hole every inch or so by backing the drill bit almost completely out of the hole with the drill still running. This will prevent sawdust from clogging the spirals in the drill bit.

5 When your hole is complete, remove the drill while it is still spinning.

Zany Wooden Toys that *Whiz, Spin, Pop, and Fly*

CONNECTING WOOD

You will often be faced with the question of how to connect one piece of wood to another. The three basic methods are nailing, screwing, and gluing. (I put gluing last because when you're inventing something, you don't want to disrupt your creativity and excitement by having to wait for glue to dry.) Knowing the advantages and disadvantages of each method will help you choose what's right for your project.

Nailing

Nails are the most common way of connecting one piece of wood to another. This method of connecting relies on the friction between the wood and the nail to hold the pieces together. Nails make a quick and fairly sturdy connection. However, while they are very strong when the force on them is sideways to the nail, they are not as strong when the force is attempting to pull the nail out.

Box nails have large heads to hold the boards together. Finishing nails have small heads that are pushed below the wood surface using a nail set for a more attractive finish (if you think nail heads are ugly).

Most nails (left) have large heads to hold the wood together, but finish nails (right) have small heads so they can be pushed beneath the wood and hidden.

ADVANTAGES AND DISADVANTAGES OF NAILS	
Advantages	**Disadvantages**
Fast to use	Wood can split due to the sideways force of the nail
Reasonably strong connection	May not be strong enough; especially weak in end grain
Not permanent	Can be difficult to remove
	Pounding on your project can loosen other pieces

NAIL PROBLEMS AND SOLUTIONS	
Problem	**Solution**
Wood splits	The nail was too close to the edge. Use the claw to pull the nail out and move it farther from the edge.
Nail bends	Most likely, the hammer is hitting the nail at an angle. Make sure the handle of the hammer is parallel to the top piece.
Nail still bends	You may be hitting a knot in the wood. Move to a new location.
Nail pokes through the second piece of wood	The nail was started crooked. Turn the project upside down, and pound the tip of the nail back into the wood so you can grab the nail head with the claw. Try again using a different hole.
Your thumb hurts	If the nails are small, you might want to hold them with a needle-nose pliers.

HOW TO NAIL

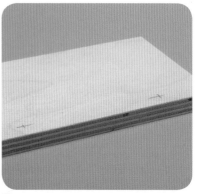

1 Choose the correct size hammer. For small projects, choose a smaller hammer (5 to 10 ounces).

2 Choose the appropriate size nail. As a rule of thumb, the nail should go into the second board about twice the thickness of the first board. For example, if you're nailing through a ¼" (6mm) board, the nail should be about ¾" (19mm) long.

3 Determine where to place each nail, and make a small mark. Don't place nails too close to the edge of a board, because the wood might split. You need to pound in at least two nails to keep the top piece from rotating. Separate the nails by about twice their length.

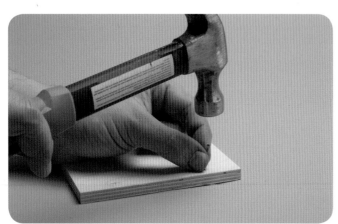

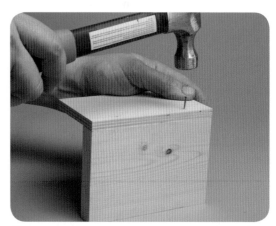

4 Start each nail in the top piece by holding it between your thumb and index finger and tapping it with the hammer. The nail should be straight up-and-down above the mark. The face of the hammer should be perpendicular to the nail. Pound in the nails just deep enough so they don't fall over.

5 Align the top piece and the bottom piece, and finish pounding in all the nails.

Screwing

Screws take a little more time than nails, but are often necessary when you want extra strength. Screws excel at pulling two pieces of wood together. The threads of the screw cut into the wood and provide extra grip—it is nearly impossible to pull out a screw. Making a hole for a typical flathead wood screw requires three different bits: one for the pilot hole, one for the clearance hole, and a countersink bit.

Screws are a secure method for attaching pieces of wood.

There are many types of screws, but for inventors, nothing beats a coarse-threaded drywall screw for ease of use and speed. If you're using short screws in softwood, such as pine, you can take a shortcut and skip all the drilling. Just make sure you hold the boards tightly together while putting in the screws. Most of the time, however, it is worth the effort to drill a clearance hole. A pilot hole may not be necessary all the time, but it will prevent the wood from splitting and make it easier to insert the screw. Drywall screws usually do a good job of countersinking themselves. If the screw head is on the bottom of your project, however, you'll want to countersink the hole to prevent the screw head from scratching any surfaces.

ADVANTAGES AND DISADVANTAGES OF SCREWS

Advantages	Disadvantages
Very strong	Drill, drill bit, and screwdriver are needed
Project can be disassembled	Slower than nailing
Pulls wood together	May need to drill three holes
No pounding on your project	

SCREW PROBLEMS AND SOLUTIONS

Problem	Solution
You've been turning for hours, and it's not going in	All screws go in clockwise. The saying is "Lefty loosey, righty tighty."
It's very hard to turn	You may have made the pilot hole too small. Before you get out the drill, try rubbing a little bar soap on the screw and putting the screw in again.
The screw keeps turning	The pilot hole is too wide, so the threads don't have enough wood to grab. Put a splinter of wood about the size of a wooden match in the hole, and try putting the screw in again.

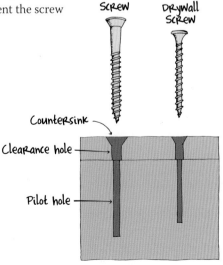

To insert a screw, you usually need to drill a pilot hole, a clearance hole, and a countersink.

Zany Wooden Toys that Whiz, Spin, Pop, and Fly

HOW TO INSERT A SCREW

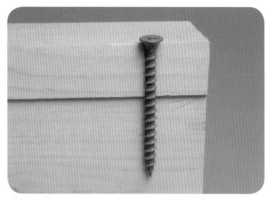

1 Choose the correct size screw. The rule of thumb for a nail also applies for a screw: It should go into the second board about twice the thickness of the first board. That's one-third in the top board and two-thirds in the bottom board.

2 Align the pieces, and drill the pilot hole. To determine the size of the pilot hole, hold a small drill bit in front of the screw. The drill bit should cover only the solid metal portion between the threads. The pilot hole also should be slightly shorter than the screw. You can mark this depth on the drill bit using a piece of tape.

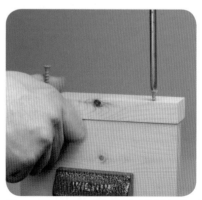

3 Drill the clearance hole through the top piece. The clearance hole is the width of the body of the screw. The screw should be able to pass through this hole without having to be turned. To determine the size of the clearance hole, hold a bit in front of the screw. This time, the drill bit should just cover the threads.

4 Drill the countersink hole. This hole is made so the head of the screw is below the level of the wood. Use a countersink bit, and apply just enough pressure to make a small indentation.

5 Use a Phillips (cross) or standard (flat) screwdriver to insert the screw. Screw it in until the boards are held together tightly.

Zany Wooden Toys that Whiz, Spin, Pop, and Fly

Gluing

Argh! I hate glue because it is so slooow. However, it does work well for holding wood together, and there are times when only glue will work. There are many different types of glue, including white glue, yellow glue, hot glue, and epoxy. White glue is what you typically buy for the first day of school. It works great on wood. If you go to a hardware store, buy yellow glue—the fancy name is aliphatic resin glue. It dries a little quicker than white glue. Both wash up with water, which is nice. Don't mess with other glues until your invention calls out for a superstrong, waterproof joint.

Glue is a secure fastener, but it often takes a long time to dry.

ADVANTAGES AND DISADVANTAGES OF GLUE	
Advantages	**Disadvantages**
Very strong connection	Slow
Can be used on very small pieces	Cannot be disassembled
Gives you time to clean up the shop	Requires clamping

GLUE PROBLEMS AND SOLUTIONS	
Problem	**Solution**
You don't have clamps	Try using rubber bands or putting weight, such as books or tools, on the pieces.
The glue dried, and the boards are in the wrong position	Start over.
You got bored waiting for the glue to dry and invented something else	Way to go!

HOW TO GLUE

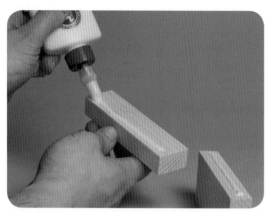

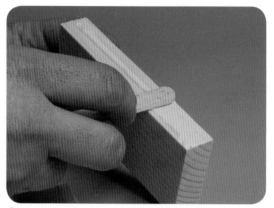

1 Make sure that the two surfaces to be glued are clean and free of oil, dirt, sawdust, or other stuff. Apply a small amount of glue to both surfaces.

2 Spread out the glue so it completely covers the surface. I like to use my finger, but you can also use a brush or a craft stick.

3 Align the pieces, and then hold them together using clamps. Apply just enough force to squeeze glue out on all sides. Fine woodworkers remove the extra glue after it has dried so that it doesn't interfere with the finish. Inventors wipe it up immediately because big blobs of glue take forever to dry.

Zany Wooden Toys that *Whiz, Spin, Pop,* and *Fly*

DECORATING AND FINISHING

Decorating a project can be just as much fun as building it and playing with it. Decorating allows you to make your toy unique, whimsical, and interesting. You can put a little of your own personality and attitude into the toy. Don't underestimate the power of decorating to bring just as many smiles as the toy itself.

So now for the last crazy woodworking word: finish. A finish is a protective coating put on the wood to help preserve it and to bring out the beauty of the wood. There are many different types of finishes, and finishing a project can be very quick or can take a few days. Knowing the basics will help you choose the finish that's right for your project. When you finish finishing your project, you are truly finished.

Decorating and finishing are absolutely not necessary. I have yet to meet a kid who wants to wait around for paint or varnish to dry on a toy he or she just made.

Painting

Acrylic paints from a hobby store or an art store work very well on wood and come in an almost infinite variety of colors. These paints dry quickly and conveniently clean up with soap and water. A basic set of red, blue, and yellow will get you started. I also like to get orange, purple, and green so I don't have to mix those colors. These paints can be watered down so that they act more like stain and show the wood grain. Either way, you'll have a very colorful and fun project.

Kid-Friendly Decorating
If you're making toys with a little kid, let him or her do the decorating. Crayons, markers, and colored pencils work great on bare wood. These have an added benefit in that they will not interfere with moving parts.

Acrylic paints and stains are great for decorating your project.

HOW TO PAINT

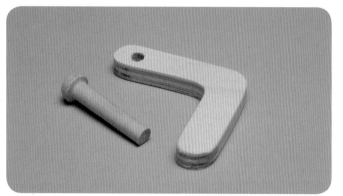

1 Disassemble the project if there are moving parts. Paint can act like glue and make moving parts stick. It is wise to paint the pieces separately.

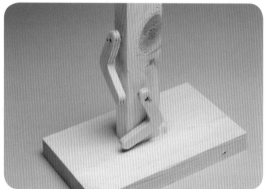

2 Make a stand or lay out scrap wood to hold your project while it dries.

3 Get a glass of water for cleaning your brush and a few paper towels for drying it off. Then, squeeze a small amount of paint onto a paper plate.

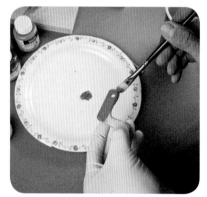

4 Apply the first color by brushing on the paint in the direction of the grain. Let this layer dry before applying the next color to prevent mixing of colors.

5 Rinse your brush in the water until it leaves no color on the paper towel when you dry it. Add the next color. Don't forget to clean the brush in warm, soapy water when you're done painting. Work the bristles sideways to remove the paint; don't mash the bristles up and down. Lay the paintbrush on its side to dry.

Finishing

There are many different types of finishes available, including oils, varnishes, shellacs, and lacquers. The two easiest finishes to use are mineral oil and water-based finish. Mineral oil is applied by using a cloth to rub it on the wood. This is a nontoxic finish, so it's safe for young kids. Water-based finish provides a warm, clear finish that brings out the natural beauty of the wood. It is applied just like paint. Whichever water-based finish you choose, be mindful of potential health hazards with fumes or with the finish itself. Nontoxic paints and finishes, such as salad bowl finishes, can be found at specialty woodworking stores. Follow the directions on the product you choose, and you'll have a beautiful and safe toy.

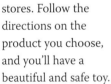

Finishes, such as salad bowl finish (left), polyurethane (middle), and butcher block oil (right), will put a nice shine on your project.

HOW TO USE A WATER-BASED FINISH

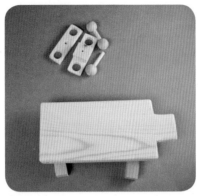

1 Disassemble the project if there are moving parts. Finish can act like glue and make moving parts stick. Lay out scraps of wood to hold your project while it dries.

2 Open the finish, and stir it with a paint stick. Do not shake the finish, because this will create bubbles and leave your finish bumpy.

3 Apply a layer of finish by brushing it on in the direction of the grain. Be careful to watch for drips at the edges.

4 Use very fine 000 or 0000 steel wool to rub down and smooth out the first layer of finish after it has thoroughly dried. Repeat Steps 2 and 3 for the second coat of finish. NOTE: See page 216 for instructions on how to clean your brush when you are done.

TOY-MAKING BASICS

You never know when an idea is going to pop into your head, so you should always be ready with a few supplies and basic toy-making know-how.

Toy-making supplies

Basic toy-making supplies can be found at many hobby stores and woodworking supply stores. Here is what I always try to keep on hand:

- 1" (25mm) and 2" (51mm) wooden wheels with ¼" (6mm) holes
- ¾" (19mm) and 1" (25mm) wooden balls (with and without holes)
- ¼" (6mm) pegs
- ¼" (6mm) dowel caps
- Craft sticks (narrow and wide)
- Hook screws
- Eye screws
- Variety of nails
- Variety of screws
- Variety of rubber bands
- Clothespins
- Wood glue
- Duct tape
- Nylon string
- Cotton string

Always have some basic toy-making supplies on hand just in case you get a sudden bright idea.

Zany Wooden Toys that *Whiz, Spin, Pop,* and *Fly*

Making Wheels

When it comes to making wheels, I prefer to use my wallet—that is, buy them at a hobby store. Manufactured wheels come in a variety of sizes and are inexpensive. The wheels with ¼" (6mm) holes are the most common. However, there are several easy ways to make wheels for your toys when going to the store is not an option.

The easiest way to make a wheel is to just cut off a section of a dowel and drill a hole in the center. You can also use a compass to draw a circle on a board, and then cut it out with a coping saw. A hole cutter for your drill will also produce nice round wheels. Your homemade wheels will probably wobble because either the hole is not dead-center or the wheel is not quite round. Don't worry about it. Nobody will ever know, because the toy is going to be played with in a sandbox, in the backyard, or on the carpet.

You can make a wheel by drawing a circle on a board and cutting it out with a coping saw.

A good method for wheel making is to slice a section from a dowel and drill a hole in the middle.

A hole-cutting bit on your power drill will make good wheels.

Making axles

Manufactured wheels are typically made with a ¼" (6mm) hole. The diameter of pegs is usually ⁷⁄₃₂" (5.5mm). Thus, the wheel will rotate freely on the peg. To quickly mount a wheel, drill a ⁷⁄₃₂" (5.5mm) hole in the project where you want the wheel, and use a peg to attach the wheel. Don't pound the peg all the way in, or it will prevent the wheel from spinning. To make an axle, drill a ⁵⁄₁₆" (8mm) hole (slightly larger than a ¼" [6mm] dowel) through the wood. Use a piece of ¼" (6mm) dowel as the axle, and mount the wheels on either side.

Lubricating Wood

Usually, when you are making action toys out of wood, there will be places where one piece of wood rubs against another. This is often the case with latches, axles, gears, levers, and similar parts. Too much friction between the pieces can make the toy difficult or impossible to play with. The first way to reduce friction is to make sure you sand both pieces smooth. If there's still too much friction, you'll need to add a lubricant. Do not use oil! The wood will absorb the oil, swell, and make matters worse. Instead, try graphite or powdered Teflon. The quickest source for graphite is the end of your pencil. Just rub a little on the two surfaces, and everything should start moving again. You can also buy tubes or bottles of powdered graphite and Teflon.

Graphite and other powdered lubricants are available commercially.

You can use a ⁷⁄₃₂" (5.5mm) peg to attach wheels by pounding the peg partially in with a hammer.

If you want to use a ¼" (6mm) dowel as an axle, drill a ⁵⁄₁₆" (8mm) hole through the wood.

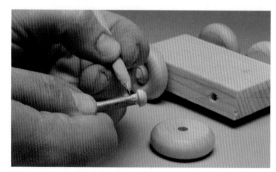

The easiest way to lubricate a moving part on a toy is to rub a pencil tip on both surfaces.

Time-saving tips

A key component to inventing toys is speed. Whether you're building with a kid or trying to capture your own idea, time is of the essence. Here are some tips on saving time.

1. Try to design toys that do not require gluing. Always consider nails, screws, and snug-fitting pegs before deciding to use glue.

2. Don't measure everything. Very few dimensions are critical. Most dimensions can just be eyeballed or estimated. For example, you can easily guess where the middle of a board is.

3. Most cuts don't have to be perfectly square. So rather than measuring a length and then using a square to lay out a perfectly straight, 90° line, just free-hand cut the board based on your one little pencil mark.

4. Drill all holes first. Review all of the holes needed so you don't have to keep changing bits.

5. Skip the internal cuts. Internal cuts take time because you have to drill a hole, disconnect the saw blade, insert it into the hole, and then reconnect it. Some of the toys in this book show internal cuts (Warp-Speed Penny Shooter Step-by-Step, page 12; Quarter Flipper, page 76; and the Ultimate Adventurer's Vehicle, page 124). These cuts are absolutely not necessary. Just cut in from the end if you want to save time. You might try a zig-zag or an S-curve to make it look interesting.

6. Take advantage of the set dimensions of common lumber. For example, say you want to draw a line down the middle of a 1" (25mm) x 2" (51mm) board. You remember that the board is actually ¾" (19mm) x 1½" (38mm). The center of the 1 x 2 is ¾" (19mm). Thus, you can mark the center of the board by just using the ¾" (19mm) width of another board.

7. Find the center of a board by drawing straight lines from each corner to the opposite corner. Where the two lines cross is dead-center.

A good example for making a toy quickly is the Warp-Speed Penny Shooter on page 13. There's really nothing that needs to be measured for this toy. The width of the board is whatever you have. The depth of the hole is however deep your drill bit can go. After drilling the hole, insert a dowel to see how deep it went, and transfer this to the top of the board. Cut the board about a penny's width longer, and proceed.

Safety

- Always wear eye protection when using cutting tools.

- Always wear ear protection when using power tools.

- Keep your fingers away from drills, blades, and other cutting edges.

- Clamp small pieces and spheres. Don't try to hold them in your hands when cutting or sawing.

- Use good ventilation when finishing your projects.

- Take good care of your tools so they'll work properly.

- Keep your work area clean.

- Don't rush.

- Keep toys with small pieces away from small children.

- If you make a toy that launches, shoots, pushes, flips, or somehow moves, make sure no one, including yourself, is in the way.

Working with small children

Kids love to build toys, and they love to help out in any way possible. Toy making is a great opportunity to teach, talk, laugh, and have fun together. A key to building toys with kids is combining simple directions with lots of patience. What's obvious to an experienced woodworker can be totally foreign to a child. Phrases such as "Mark a square line" and "Hand me the bit" combine words that don't make any sense in their world. Take the time to teach them and show them now, and you'll have a helpful assistant in no time at all.

Here are some steps of the toy-making process that kids can help with. As always, direct supervision is recommended.

- Carrying wood

- Marking and measuring

- Cutting with handsaws (with direct supervision)

- Clamping: Kids can help with either holding the clamp or twisting the handle.

- Nailing: Make sure the helper uses needle-nose pliers to hold the nail. Otherwise, their fingers are likely to take as many hits as the nail.

- Pounding in pegs: Have the child place a piece of cardboard under the wheels to prevent the peg from being hammered all the way in.

- Inserting screws

- Squeezing and spreading glue

- Inserting rubber bands

- Sanding

- Decorating with crayons, markers, and colored pencils

U.S. to Metric Conversion

To convert from U.S. measurements to metric, use the chart below. If the U.S. measurement is greater than 1", multiply the number of inches by 25.4mm, add any fractions, and round to the nearest .5mm.

Example: 5⅝"

5" x 25.4mm = 127mm

⅝" = 16mm

127mm + 16mm = 143mm

CONVERSION CHART

U.S. Measurements	Metric
¹⁄₁₆"	2mm
³⁄₃₂"	2.5mm
⅛"	3mm
⅙"	4mm
⁵⁄₃₂"	4mm
³⁄₁₆"	5mm
⁷⁄₃₂"	5.5mm
¼"	6mm
⁹⁄₃₂"	7mm
⁵⁄₁₆"	8mm
⅜"	10mm
⁷⁄₁₆"	11mm
¹⁵⁄₃₂"	12mm
½"	13mm
⅝"	16mm
¾"	19mm
⅞"	22mm
1"	25mm

INDEX

More Great Project Books from Fox Chapel Publishing

Great Book of Wooden Toys
More Than 50 Easy-to-Build Projects
By Norm Marshall

More than 50 easy-to-follow projects for building classic wooden toys, including a Model T car, a bulldozer, steam engine, biplane, and many more.

ISBN: 978-1-56523-431-4
$19.95 • 232 Pages

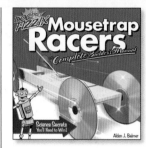

Doc Fizzix Mousetrap Racers
By Alden Balmer

Learn to build winning mousetrap-powered vehicles like Little Moe and Speed Trap. Also includes a bonus science fair project and easy-to-understand explanations of physics concepts.

ISBN: 978-1-56523-359-1
$14.95 • 144 Pages

Turning Vintage Toys
By Chris Reid

Make timeless toys from the Victorian and Edwardian eras with 15 projects for toy soldiers, quoits, skittles, a juggling diabolo, and many more.

ISBN: 978-1-56523-451-2
$24.95 • 192 Pages

Kid Crafts: Woodworking
By John Kelsey

Introduce woodworking to the next generation with 10 projects that only require ordinary lumber and simple hand tools. Learn to build a bird nesting box, tool box, and much more.

ISBN: 978-1-56523-353-9
$12.95 • 104 Pages

Making Furniture and Dollhouses for American Girl and Other 18-Inch Dolls: Revised and Expanded Second Edition
By Dennis Simmons

Learn to create an heirloom quality dollhouse and furniture for the ever-popular American Girl and other 18" dolls.

ISBN: 978-1-56523-402-4
$24.95 • 200 Pages

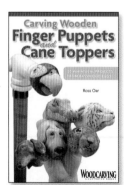

Carving Wooden Finger Puppets and Cane Toppers
By Ross Oar

Easy-to-make and inexpensive, basswood egg puppets are fun carving projects. Includes two projects for Freddy the Frog and Tom Cat, as well as 11 additional patterns.

ISBN: 978-1-56523-389-8
$14.95 • 80 Pages

Look For These Books at Your Local Bookstore or Woodworking Retailer
To order direct, call **800-457-9112** or visit *www.FoxChapelPublishing.com*

By mail, please send check or money order + $4.00 per book for S&H to: Fox Chapel Publishing, 1970 Broad Street, East Petersburg, PA 17520